REIMAGINING BUSINESS SCHOOLS FOR THE 21ST CENTURY

Manchester University Press

REIMAGINING BUSINESS SCHOOLS FOR THE 21ST CENTURY

Alliance Manchester Business School

Edited by Ken McPhail

with Jim Pendrill

MANCHESTER UNIVERSITY PRESS

Copyright © Manchester University Press 2025

While copyright in the volume as a whole is vested in Manchester University Press, copyright in individual chapters belongs to their respective authors, and no chapter may be reproduced wholly or in part without the express permission in writing of both author and publisher.

Published by Manchester University Press
Oxford Road, Manchester, M13 9PL

www.manchesteruniversitypress.co.uk

British Library Cataloguing-in-Publication Data
A catalogue record for this book is available from the British Library

ISBN 978 1 5261 9339 1   hardback

First published 2025

The publisher has no responsibility for the persistence or accuracy of URLs for any external or third-party internet websites referred to in this book, and does not guarantee that any content on such websites is, or will remain, accurate or appropriate.

EU authorised representative for GPSR:
Easy Access System Europe, Mustamäe tee 50, 10621 Tallinn, Estonia
gpsr.requests@easproject.com

Typeset
by New Best-set Typesetters Ltd
Printed in Great Britain
by Bell & Bain Ltd, Glasgow

CONTENTS

List of plates	*page* vii
List of figures and table	ix
List of contributors	xi
Foreword	xiii
Fiona Devine	
Preface: Evolution of the Alliance Manchester Business School	xv
Luke Georghiou	
List of abbreviations	xxxiv
Introduction: The role of business schools in universities, the economy and society	1
Duncan Ivison and Ken McPhail	
1 Navigating the net zero transition	12
Frank W. Geels and Sacha Sadan	
2 Catalysing Manchester's innovation ecosystem to unlock economic growth	27
Lou Cordwell	
3 Cities, regions and turning around the North	41
Terry Leahy and Philip McCann	

4 The future of finance: financial technology and
   innovation for growth   61
   Catherine L. Mann and Markos Zachariadis
5 The importance of management and leadership for
   better wellbeing and productivity in the workplace   77
   Cary Cooper and Tera Allas
6 Tackling economic and societal challenges in Greater
   Manchester: the role of the University of Manchester
   and Alliance Manchester Business School   93
   Jill Rubery and Andrew Westwood
7 Red pill or blue pill? Do we shape AI's future, or do we
   allow it to shape us?   106
   Michelle Carter and Richard Allmendinger
8 The creativity crisis in business schools: business,
   imagination and creativity   119
   John McAuliffe and Bruce S. Tether
9 What is the point of business school research? Reflecting
   on six decades of achievement at the University of
   Manchester and the adaptive challenges ahead   132
   Gerard P. Hodgkinson and Elvira Uyarra
10 The global business school in a 'slowbalised' world   146
   Peter J. Buckley and Axèle Giroud
Conclusion: A business school for the twenty-first century   160
   Fiona Devine and Nazir Afzal

Index   173

PLATES

1 Main entrance to AMBS (AMBS/James Maddox)
2 Executive Education Centre AMBS (AMBS/James Maddox)
3 The front plaza of AMBS (AMBS/James Maddox)
4 Early days of redevelopment of AMBS (BDP/Nick Caville)
5 Aerial shot of AMBS redevelopment looking east across the University of Manchester campus (BDP/Nick Caville)
6 The interior of AMBS during reconstruction (BDP/Nick Caville)
7 The main stairway and student area during redevelopment (BDP/Nick Caville)
8 AMBS today looking towards the Eddie Davies Library (BDP/Nick Caville)
9 The main internal concourse of AMBS (BDP/Nick Caville)
10 The dazzling frontage of AMBS (BDP/Nick Caville)
11 Library space in AMBS (BDP/Nick Caville)
12 What Manchester Means. Wall inside the entrance to AMBS Executive Education Centre (AMBS/James Maddox)
13 The main open-plan learning space of AMBS (BDP/Nick Caville)
14 AMBS staff join construction workers for the topping-out ceremony of the new building (AMBS/Bernadette Delaney)

15 Professor Fiona Devine, then Head of AMBS, plants a tree during the topping-out ceremony (AMBS/Bernadette Delaney)
16 Lord Alliance (pictured to the right of Professor Fiona Devine) and Eddie Davies (to her left) join AMBS staff to celebrate the new building (AMBS/Bernadette Delaney)

FIGURES AND TABLE

Figures

1.1 Structural changes for net zero transitions. Chart supported by NapkinAI, March 2025   *page* 15
1.2 Annual global CO_2 emissions (in billion tonnes) per region, 1950–2022. Constructed using data from Our World in Data, *CO_2 and Greenhouse Gas Emissions Data Explorer*, https://ourworldindata.org/explorers/co2   17
1.3 Share of electricity production from renewables (in percentages) in Europe, the US, China, Germany and the UK, 1985–2023. Constructed using data from Our World in Data, *Renewable Energy*, https://ourworldindata.org/renewable-energy   17
1.4 Annual domestic sales of EVs (in millions) in China, Europe and the US, 2010–23. Constructed using data from IEA (2024) *Global EV Outlook 2024: Moving Towards Increased Affordability*, Paris: International Energy Agency.   18
1.5 Annual domestic sales of BEVs as percentage of market share in China, Europe and the US, 2010–23. Constructed using data from IEA (2024) *Global EV*

     Outlook 2024: Moving Towards Increased Affordability, Paris:
     International Energy Agency.   19
1.6 Global weighted average levelised cost of electricity
     for solar-PV, offshore wind and onshore wind, 2010–
     22, in 2022 US$/kWh. Constructed using data from
     IRENA (2023) *Renewable Power Generation Costs in 2022*,
     Abu Dhabi: International Renewable Energy Agency   20
10.1 The governance triangle model – global pressures on
     university business schools   147

Table

P.1 Directors and Heads of the Business School,
     1965–2025   xx

CONTRIBUTORS

Nazir Afzal, Chancellor of the University of Manchester.
Tera Allas CBE, Chair, Pro Bono Economics and Honorary Professor, Alliance Manchester Business School.
Richard Allmendinger, Professor of Applied Artificial Intelligence, Alliance Manchester Business School.
Peter J. Buckley, 200th Anniversary Chair in International Business, Alliance Manchester Business School.
Michelle Carter, Professor of Information Systems, Alliance Manchester Business School.
Sir Cary Cooper, 50th Anniversary Professor of Organisational Psychology and Health, Alliance Manchester Business School.
Lou Cordwell, CEO of Unit M and Professor of Innovation and Special Advisor to the Office of the President and Vice-Chancellor, University of Manchester.
Fiona Devine, Vice-President and Dean, Faculty of Humanities, University of Manchester.
Frank W. Geels, Eddie Davies Professor of Sustainability Transitions, Alliance Manchester Business School.
Luke Georghiou, Professor of Science and Technology Policy and Management and Associate Vice-President, University of Manchester.

Axèle Giroud, Professor of International Business, Alliance Manchester Business School.
Gerard P. Hodgkinson, Professor of Strategic Management and Behavioural Science, Alliance Manchester Business School.
Duncan Ivison, President and Vice-Chancellor, University of Manchester.
Sir Terry Leahy, Alliance Manchester Business School alumnus and former Chancellor of the University of Manchester.
Catherine L. Mann, Honorary Professor, Alliance Manchester Business School, Professor of Practice, Brandeis University, and external member of the Bank of England Monetary Policy Committee.
John McAuliffe, Professor of Poetry, and Director Creative Manchester, University of Manchester.
Philip McCann, Sir Terry Leahy Chair in Urban and Regional Economics, Alliance Manchester Business School.
Ken McPhail, Head of Alliance Manchester Business School.
Jill Rubery, Professor of Comparative Employment Systems, Alliance Manchester Business School.
Sacha Sadan, Director of Sustainable Finance, Financial Conduct Authority and Honorary Professor, Alliance Manchester Business School.
Bruce S. Tether, Professor of Innovation Management and Strategy, Alliance Manchester Business School.
Elvira Uyarra, Professor of Innovation Studies, Alliance Manchester Business School.
Andrew Westwood, Professor of Government Practice, University of Manchester.
Markos Zachariadis, Chair of Financial Technology (FinTech) and Information Systems and Founding Director of the Centre for Financial Technology Studies, Alliance Manchester Business School.

FOREWORD

Fiona Devine

This book is dedicated to the memory of Lord David Alliance CBE. He was a visionary whose belief in the transformative power of education will forever serve to shape our mission, ambition and community for the future. Lord Alliance was not simply a supporter of business education. He was a catalyst for its evolution. He led the way.

I was fortunate enough to know Lord Alliance during his lifetime, and to witness his extraordinary gift to the School in 2015. His belief in the power of education, research and leadership to fuel meaningful change was more than philanthropic. It was deeply grounded in values we continue to uphold. The renaming of the School stands as a testament to his legacy and will endure as a symbol of forward momentum, possibility and purpose.

Throughout his life, Lord Alliance championed the belief that education and research are among the most powerful tools for social and economic advancement. His impact extended far beyond the Alliance Manchester Business School. He was an early supporter of the University of Manchester Institute of Science and Technology and invested in life sciences, law and international research. His influence touched disciplines, communities and generations across The University of Manchester and beyond.

He understood that business education must do more than equip students with knowledge. It must cultivate curiosity, courage and a commitment to inclusive leadership. His entrepreneurial spirit continues to inspire our pursuit of innovation and global impact. As we reimagine the future of business education in these pages, we carry forward Lord Alliance's enduring commitment to progress.

In dedicating this book to Lord David Alliance, we honour not only what he made possible, but also the future he imagined where education is a force for good and business is a vehicle for positive change. His legacy lives on in the aspirations of every student, the vision of our academics and the work of each changemaker shaped by the Alliance Manchester Business School.

PREFACE: EVOLUTION OF THE ALLIANCE MANCHESTER BUSINESS SCHOOL

Luke Georghiou

The history of the Alliance Manchester Business School (AMBS), which marked its sixtieth anniversary in 2025, is closely intertwined with that of the University of Manchester, of which it is part, and of business and management-related education and research in the University's predecessor institutions, the Victoria University of Manchester (VUM) and the University of Manchester Institute of Science and Technology (UMIST). The story is also one of the interaction between the needs of businesses and those who work in them for management education and research and the challenge of accommodating a subject which was perceived by many of its practitioners as having distinctive needs. Over the six decades some saw this requirement as demanding substantial variation from the norms of university governance and finance. This tension has governed the evolution of AMBS. Such processes are rarely complete and new challenges are always around the corner, but, as we mark the diamond jubilee, its founders would likely be astounded by the scale, scope and quality of the world-class business school that is AMBS today.

Origins and antecedents

A full understanding of the origins of today's entity needs to begin by tracing back the four elements of VUM and UMIST which were combined to form the School during the merger of the universities in 2004.[1] The longest tradition of management education in Manchester belonged to UMIST. In its initial identity as the Manchester Municipal Technical School, it had formed a Faculty of Commerce and Administration, replaced at the end of the Great War by a Department of Industrial Administration in what was by then called the Manchester College of Technology. A precarious financial existence was sustained by sporadic donations and grants from businesses, individuals and foundations.[2] Industrial Administration continued until 1965, when it was renamed the Department of Management Sciences.[3] A contemporary review of a volume of eight lectures given there stated,

> All of the papers, however, are dealing with some phase of the administration of the human problems in industry and are concerned with the management of men rather than with the management of machines, materials, finished products – or with such topics as 'cost-accounting,' 'routing' or scientific management in the narrow sense.[4]

Thus, even at this early stage a focus on human aspects of management characterised the UMIST School. The Department's first Director, A. F. Kent, was an industrial psychologist recruited from the University of Bristol. This capability endured such that in the 2004 merger Manchester School of Management (MSM) staff formed the core of the current School's People, Management and Organisation division. In the meantime, MSM had extended its base to cover the full range of management disciplines. In part the function had been to provide technologists with management education to enable their progression from technical to senior general roles in business.[5] An influential recruit to the chair of management was Reginald 'Reg' Revans, who joined the Department of Management Sciences in 1955. A polymath who had studied astrophysics at the Cavendish Laboratory, then under Ernest Rutherford, he also worked with Teddy Chester, the VUM management education pioneer. His principal contribution to management studies was Action Learning, a problem-solving approach in which practitioners take action and reflect upon the results.[6]

Coinciding with its change of name, in 1965 under the leadership of Ronald Beresford Dew, the Department launched the nation's first undergraduate programme in management sciences as well, going on to provide a series of specialist masters degrees and doctoral education. In 1998 the Department was again renamed, as the Manchester School of Management. The transformation to research excellence was driven by Roland Smith (later Sir Roland) the country's first Professor of Marketing, organisational psychologist Sir Cary Cooper (see Chapter 5) who later served as UMIST Deputy Vice-Chancellor, long serving head of School John Goodman, logistics pioneer Bob Hollier, and influential gender and labour markets expert Jill Rubery (see Chapter 6). Industrial innovation expert Rod Coombs, as UMIST Pro-Vice Chancellor, played a part in initiating the Manchester merger and went on to become Deputy President of the University of Manchester.

Three parts of the School had their origins in the Victoria University of Manchester's Faculty of Economic and Social Studies (FESS),[7] albeit separated by a period of almost forty years. The foundation of the original Manchester Business School (MBS), the sixtieth anniversary marked by the publication of this volume, began this evolution. John Williams's authoritative history of MBS in the years up to 1990 describes how senior academics in the Faculty, who had since the 1950s published influential research on business and/or delivered management education, provided the groundwork and impetus.[8] Probably the most important of these were Bruce Williams (latterly knighted and Vice-Chancellor of the University of Sydney), who held the Stanley Jevons Chair of Political Economy, and Teddy Chester, Professor of Social Administration, who had initiated the University's first management course in 1956, which was targeted from the beginning at senior business managers and was also the foundation of a long-term capability in health services management. They were joined from the University of Sheffield by economist Douglas Hague (subsequently a close adviser of Margaret Thatcher and Chairman of the Economic and Social Research Council), who was recruited to lead management education in the Faculty.[9] The vehicle for this was a newly created Manchester School of Management and Administration, variously abbreviated as Mansma and MANSMAN.[10] It was essentially a coordinating committee, but nonetheless enabled a postgraduate Diploma in Management Studies to be launched in 1963. This assembly of academics of high standing and a proto-management school served the University well when a national need for management education was perceived.

The backdrop was a feeling that Britain's industrial underperformance was at least partly caused by business leadership being dominated by family businesses and a general antipathy towards recruiting managers from specialised as opposed to generalist higher education, in contrast to the US tradition of business schools epitomised by the likes of Harvard Business School. Following an influential report on the future of higher education chaired by Lord Robbins which called for the foundation of two business schools,[11] a further inquiry was instituted and headed by Lord Franks, who, among his other roles, was Chairman of Lloyds Bank. His remit was 'to formulate a plan and select a suitable university or universities for the furtherance of management education in Britain'.[12] The recommendation was for one business school to be situated in London (the origin of London Business School – LBS) and the second in Manchester. The chosen base was the activities emerging from FESS rather than the Department of Industrial Administration, possibly because of the stronger national connections and academic reputations of its leading proponents and an already existing commitment to joint research with business through a Centre for Business Research, which was to become part of the School. Thus, Manchester would have two centres for management education but with very different emphases. Over the years there was a mutually recognised and very rarely breached convention that the Department at UMIST would not use the word 'business' in its degree titles, while the Business School would not use the word 'management'.

After beginning its activities under the wing of FESS, the formal establishment of Manchester Business School was as the Faculty of Business Administration from January 1968, the same year that the degree of Master of Business Administration was launched. Described by Pullan as a 'strange hybrid',[13] the structure was distinct from that of the other faculties and evolved to be governed by a Council presided over by the Vice-Chancellor and consisting of eight members of Senate, nine leading lights of industry and one trade unionist.[14] Franks had seen this joint governance of policy and money as a means of balancing the influence of university and business, but the passage of time would reveal significant tensions. The relationship with the rest of the University has been a recurrent theme only fully resolved in recent years.

Funding at this stage came from a recurrent grant from the University Grants Committee (UGC) and a matching amount raised from British business via a trust called the Foundation for Management Education (FME). This arrangement stemmed from a recommendation by the Normanbrook working party established by the Federation of British Industries to address the financial implications of the Franks report.[15] By 1972 the UGC grant and FME funding each contributed 25 per cent of the School's income, with 10 per cent from course fees and 20 per cent from research grants, the remaining 10 per cent coming from diverse sources. Direct funding for MBS and LBS from the UGC's successor, the Universities Funding Council, ended in 1992.

Directors of MBS pre-merger

In many ways the history of the Business School can be marked by the terms of office of its eight Directors and Heads to date, shown in Table P.1, of whom four were in the pre-merger era and three after, with John Arnold spanning the change.[16]

A head-hunting exercise led to the appointment in 1965 of Grigor McClelland as the founding Director of MBS. McClelland combined an academic background with direct business experience in his family's retail business, Laws Stores. McClelland had an enormous formative influence on the School. He had been involved with both the Franks and Normanbrook committees, bringing a strong commitment to the national project. Possibly stemming from his Quaker beliefs, McClelland had a strong commitment to social responsibility in business, anticipating the University's elevation of that goal by half a century.

Table P.1 Directors and Heads of the Business School, 1965–2025

Director	Term of office
W. Grigor McClelland	1965–77
Tom Lupton	1977–84
Rab Telfer	1984–88
Tom Cannon	1989–93
John Arnold	1994–2007
Mike Luger	2007–13
Fiona Devine	2013–23
Ken McPhail	2023–

Note: Excludes interim appointees Richard Stapleton (1984) and Tony Cockerill (1993) and the collective leadership by the heads of the four Federal School partners during the merger transition (2004).

His management style was collegiate and flexible, reflected in a decision to avoid having departments in the School.

McClelland's main contribution to teaching was what is variously referred to as 'The Manchester Experiment' and, in recent years, 'The Manchester Method'. This was intended to combine intensive study of theory and development of critical thinking with a 'learning-by-doing' approach based on projects and case studies. This had some similarities to the action-learning approach of Revans in that both used experiential learning and addressed real-life contemporary business problems, but the Manchester Method was designed for use in the structured environment of business education. An e-book by Tudor Rickards, at MBS from 1972 until his move to Emeritus status in 2008, as MBS's Professor of Creativity and Organisational Change, reviewed the method's origins and significance.[17] The book gives credit for the approach to pioneering academics in the early days of the School. Two of the most celebrated were cybernetics guru Stafford Beer and socio-technical systems pioneer Enid Mumford. Mumford was commemorated in the University of Manchester's 200th anniversary installation, Bicentenary Way, as the first woman to hold a full professorship at a UK business school. Her achievement highlighted the extreme gender imbalance of the early days of business education. The Manchester Method, with its team-based approach, continues today to characterise the School's approach to the MBA degree in particular.

A thirteen-month gap followed McClelland's return to his family business, after which a founding professor Tom Lupton was elevated from the Deputy Director post. His time in office was marked by substantial growth (a 250 per cent increase in income) and by internationalisation of the student population, which by the early 1980s hailed from some seventy countries. Nonetheless, the financial outlook continued to be risk prone, especially with the prospect of the end of direct grant funding and dependence on the potentially volatile MBA and executive education markets. A review of the relationship between MBS and the University immediately after Lupton's retirement in 1983 reaffirmed that the School should remain an integral part, but also that it should be financially independent, on the understanding that the University would underwrite it if a serious problem arose.

Lupton's successor, Rab Telfer, came from a senior business executive background but nonetheless recognised criticisms of the School's academic standing and sought to raise it through external appointments (with only limited success) and encouraging the raising of research grants. Nonetheless, the 1989 UGC RAE (Research Assessment Exercise) yielded a low point for MBS, with a rating of 3 (out of 5).

The next director, Tom Cannon, arrived from the University of Stirling with a strong research record and a commitment to make MBS a research-driven enterprise. He set about organisational reform but became embroiled in a high-profile dispute with the University leadership when he persuaded the lay members of the School Council to request a form of legal autonomy that would maintain a link to the University via the Faculty of Business Administration but would otherwise move towards financial autonomy through a company limited by guarantee or by a charter arrangement similar to that of UMIST. This would include employment of staff and management of assets. Staff in the School were strongly divided on the topic, but reaction from the University was clear. The proposals were not acceptable and the consequence was the departure of the Director and the resignation of the entire MBS Council. However, a new momentum was emerging from this controversy.

The Federal School era

A letter dated 17 July 1991 from Deputy Vice-Chancellor S. A. Moore to all staff in MBS informed them that the University Senate had passed a motion by 105 votes for, 3 against and 1 abstention rejecting on academic grounds the proposed governance changes and stating that MBS would remain fully in the University. The motion reaffirmed Senate's support for a 'federal model' for management education in Manchester comprising MSM, MBS and Accounting and Finance. Since 1990 there had already been a joint degree in accounting between the School of Accounting and Finance and MSM. The wider plan was fully realised in 1994 with the formation of the Manchester Federal School of Business and Management. By that time a fourth partner had been included, Policy Research in Engineering Science and Technology (PREST), a research and postgraduate institute. The constituent parts would retain their own identity and institutional affiliation. It was recognised in its vision statement that the sum of the parts created a multidisciplinary, research-based, full range business and management school. For a decade the coordinating committees of the Federal School brokered a more coherent image and, to some degree, substance to management education at the Manchester institutions, but it became evident that the transaction costs of so doing were quite high.

Meanwhile, in the post-Cannon period of MBS, after a second interregnum, John Arnold moved from his Pro-Vice-Chancellor role to become the fifth Director of MBS. He was quick to undertake a comprehensive review of the School's activities, recognising the recurrent financial risks of reliance on an MBA programme and executive education that were not underpinned by revenue from a large undergraduate activity or specialist masters programmes, by contrast with key competitors. He also recognised the need to bridge a cultural divide between academic scholars and executive education specialists who did not conduct research of that nature.

Completing the merger

In the preparations for the formation of the new University of Manchester in 2004,[18] the experience and template provided by the Federal School meant that the composition of the merged business school was not contentious. Rod Coombs's experience in the Federal School of the difficulties of working with different legal entities at a micro-level may well have influenced the bold recommendation of the Beacham working party that he was a member of to recommend a full merger of VUM and UMIST rather than a collaborative model.[19]

For the School, a more active debate concerned its organisational location in the University's faculty structure. The decision to have large faculties composed of a small number of schools meant that it was unlikely that the new business school could have the status of a separate faculty that MBS had enjoyed. Despite the origins of his appointment, Arnold had become a champion of autonomy, albeit within the University structure. The leadership and staff were divided on the relative merits of retaining faculty status or being in a 'super-faculty' in combination with the remainder of the Faculty of Social Science and Law, but most reacted with some alarm when what became the final outcome was on the table, a Faculty of Humanities with an even wider disciplinary reach extending to the former Faculty of Arts. The arrival of the newly appointed Vice-President and Dean of Humanities, Professor Alistair Ulph, a distinguished economist and experienced university administrator, helped to allay these fears. The part of the School coming from MBS found itself with a stronger line of accountability than experienced in the past but also a set of interdisciplinary opportunities for engagement with economic and social challenges.

An interesting postscript to the merger lay in the naming of the School. Many staff had expected it to include both of the terms business and management to reflect the combined heritage (and the Federal

School example). A poll had also favoured this choice, but reaction from alumni of MBS was reported to be negative. With a potential market risk in the parts most sensitive to a change, the decision was taken to retain the name of Manchester Business School, albeit attached to a very different activity.

As noted, two elements of the merged School came from FSSL. The third founding pillar was built from the School of Accounting and Finance (SAF). A mainstay of FSSL since its foundation in 1968, this was expanded by the addition of cognate staff from MSM and MBS. SAF and MSM anticipated the Federal School by four years by launching a joint MSc degree in 1990. John Arnold had headed SAF until becoming a Pro-Vice-Chancellor in VUM in 1989, to be succeeded by Martin Walker, who in years to come would be MBS's Deputy Director and research lead. SAF had a secure financial base in teaching with its orientation to the profession, but was also focused on academic excellence as manifested in high-quality publications, an ambition regularly rewarded by high ratings in the RAE/Research Excellence Framework national research assessments.

The remaining element to be combined at merger, PREST, had begun its existence in 1977 as the research wing of the Department of Liberal Studies in Science, a department established in 1966 to develop individuals who bridged the gap between science and engineering and social sciences in support of regeneration of the national economy.[20] Some staff moved to Management Sciences in UMIST, including Ken Green, who was head of MSM at the time of the merger, and Rod Coombs (see above). By 1990 the staff of the original department had been redeployed to other parts of the University and the postgraduate programme taken over by PREST, which had moved from the Faculty of Science to FSSL. In a loop which was characteristic of the field, MBS founder Sir Bruce Williams returned to the UK and his academic roots as head of a new national initiative, the London-based Technical Change Centre, and established Manchester as the northern hub of its activity.

Close connections remained across the diaspora, and in 1996 a joint application by PREST and staff of the Centre for Research on

Organisations, Management and Technical Change led to the award of the Centre for Innovation and Competition (CRIC) by the Economic and Social Research Council (ESRC). Its co-leader, the pioneering economist of innovation and Stanley Jevons Professor of Political Economy, Stan Metcalfe, remained affiliated to both CRIC and PREST but retained his academic base as Professor of Economics in the School of Social Sciences. The proliferation of acronyms was rationalised when the parent and shared institutes unified as the Manchester Institute of Innovation Research (MIoIR), which at the point of merger became one of the four components making up the combined School.[21] MIoIR continues to this day as a University Institute based in AMBS. MBS had also sustained a long tradition of research on industrial innovation through its R&D Research Unit, established as early as 1967 under the leadership of Alan Pearson. Its legacy survives through the journal *R&D Management* and the associated charity RADMA. The Executive Director of PREST at the time of merger, Luke Georghiou, later followed Coombs in becoming Deputy President of the merged university (2017–24).

'Original Thinking Applied' and the Alliance Manchester Business School

Post-merger, John Arnold was confirmed as Director of the School and oversaw the early years. A search process was initiated for a successor, with the President and Vice-Chancellor Alan Gilbert particularly keen to appoint someone with leadership experience in a US business school. The selected candidate was Mike Luger, formerly Professor of Entrepreneurship and Director of the Centre for Competitive Economies at Kenan-Flagler Business School, the undergraduate and graduate business school at the University of North Carolina. During his tenure, MBS moved from deficit to a healthy surplus as early duplication from the merger was reduced. A strong marketing initiative was undertaken, including formation of a new advisory board. A branding exercise undertaken by consultants led to a new mission statement and the School's current brand essence, Original Thinking

Applied. Rickards' book includes a blog he attributes to MBA student Vikram Madinani titled 'Original Thinking Applied – is it The Manchester Method in Disguise?'[22] providing a thread from the School's early identity. The 'Original' echoes both the pioneering origin of MBS and graphic designer Peter Saville's celebrated characterisation of Manchester as the original modern city. 'Thinking' is an allusion both to research and to the qualities embodied in the School's graduates, while 'Applied' signals bringing theory into management practice, perhaps the clearest link to The Manchester Method.

In an echo of earlier events, Luger became embroiled in a new debate over the degree of autonomy the School had from the University, in this case a wish for the School to become a faculty and hence have its director reporting directly to the President and Vice-Chancellor as a member of the University leadership team. A working party in late 2009, led by Deputy President and Deputy Vice-Chancellor Dame Nancy Rothwell, recognised support for the idea from MBS staff and the Advisory Group, but it was rejected amid concerns about future financial stability in the sector and the overall interests of the University.

Luger's resignation as Director was announced in June 2013, with Fiona Devine, then Head of the School of Social Sciences and a distinguished sociologist, becoming Acting Head. Devine (see concluding chapter), the first female head, was confirmed in post by the Dean and Vice-President of Humanities, Keith Brown, the following year. While coming from a cognate academic background, her appointment signalled the University's commitment to a broader interdisciplinary engagement for the School. She was quick to engage positively with alumni and the local and global business communities. With what many would see as the strongest research standing of any director to date, she also actively pursued raising the quality of the research base in the School through a dual strategy of addressing underperformance and recruitment of leading academics, albeit in a difficult market. Among the new arrivals was her future Deputy Head and Director of Research and eventual successor, Ken McPhail, as Professor of Accounting. Her tenure also saw the major redevelopment of the

PREFACE

AMBS building, which led to the renaming of the School in honour of its principal donor, Lord Alliance.

A global footprint

AMBS is today home to one of the country's largest concentrations of international students with just under 2,500 registered in 2024/25 coming from ninety-four countries. Around ninety were doctoral researchers, with the remainder evenly split between masters and undergraduate levels. The talent and diversity they bring is much valued, as is the vital contribution of international fees. An insight on the educational value came during a Vital Topics lecture by alumnus Sean Marett, Chief Business and Commercial Officer of the German company BioNTech, famed for developing the first approved mRNA-based COVID-19 vaccine. Asked what he most valued from his MBA, he replied that it was learning how to work effectively in international teams, very much the story of BioNTech's breakthrough with his German-Turkish scientific partners.

International reach also takes place through distance- and blended-learning. Here the School had been in the vanguard of the University's efforts. An original joint venture in financial management with the University of Wales at Bangor, initiated by Professor Doug Wood, offered a Global MBA but was in financial difficulties. Bangor's 50 per cent was bought out for a notional sum by the University of Manchester in 2007. Director John Arnold brought in Nigel Banister to professionalise the operations of the subsidiary company, now named MBS Worldwide. A key distinctive part of the new offering was the opening of centres for the business in key global hubs with market potential, initially Singapore and Hong Kong, followed by a Middle East Centre in Dubai in 2006, and in 2008 by a centre in Shanghai.

The Global MBA remains the premium product but the University has seen the potential for extending the model across a range of disciplines and the company is now University of Manchester Worldwide. Its model of support and contact via the centres benefits students with busy careers and reduces travel, and the University avoids the risks of operating a full-blown overseas campus.

A story also told in buildings

The story of the Business School is also reflected in the buildings it has occupied. During the Mansma period management courses at the VUM had been taught in a mixture of University premises for graduate courses and a hotel in south Manchester for post-experience classes. Upon the formation of MBS in 1965, offices were rented in a city centre location, Hilton House, overflowing into a second building, Fourways House. This remained the School's location until 1971, when the purpose-built accommodation on Booth Street West was ready for occupation. It had been paid for out of funds raised in the original appeal to business, leading Pullen to comment that 'nobody knew for certain whether it belonged to the University or the school, and a case could be made for either proposition'.[23]

Designed by architects Cruickshank & Seward, the building was part of a larger complex, the somewhat infamous Precinct Centre designed by Wilson and Womersley. This was based on a concept of elevated walkways which were never fully completed and situated student accommodation, University and commercial buildings around a first-floor shopping centre which failed commercially. One consequence for the Business School was, as an architectural review put it, that its main entrance was 'a downplayed almost domestic-scale door on the west side of the block'.[24] Internal navigation from the School to the Precinct was complex. Over the years various efforts were made to improve the first impressions for visitors arriving at MBS, including relocation of the main entrance from Booth Street to the south side, with a drop-off area for vehicles. Some saw it as symbolic that access from the heart of the University campus became increasingly difficult.

During the Federal School period a substantial competitive grant had been secured from the Joint Infrastructure Fund, a national initiative for the renewal of university infrastructure. The grant was used to convert the student accommodation in the Precinct to premises that were mainly to accommodate PREST and CRIC. The heavily refurbished building was named in honour of the former UMIST Vice-Chancellor, Professor Harold Hankins.

Also in the time of the Federal School, the Manchester School of Management moved from the its principal home on the lower floors of the fifteen-storey Maths and Social Sciences Building on the UMIST campus. This embellished Brutalist-style building had been built in 1969. It had a second role in the history of AMBS in that MSM's successor on the lower floor, the Department of Computation, became the new University's School of Informatics post-merger. Informatics described its role as being a discipline for developing computer-based applications combined with multidisciplinary system design. Nonetheless, the School struggled to deal with falling enrolments and research challenges, leading to it, in 2007, being dissolved with staff divided between the Business School and Computer Science. The critical importance of digital transformation to business has ensured that informatics, broadly defined, remains a core part of the AMBS portfolio.

Meanwhile, in 1998 MSM moved to its new building on the corner of Booth Street East and Oxford Road. Aided by contributions from the Alliance family and other donors, the building was a prominent statement of the School's ambitions, but later encountered various practical problems. Renamed 'MBS East' post-merger, it continued to house School staff, principally those with an MSM background, before closure in 2018 and eventual refurbishment as a centre for flexible learning, which represented a major step in the University's zero carbon strategy.

A detail of the Federal School era's concentration of the partners around the Booth Street crossroads was the bridge across Booth Street East connecting MSM with Crawford House, where the Department of Accounting and Finance had relocated. Acquired second-hand, the footbridge was seen by some as a gesture of unity, but the UMIST Vice-Chancellor, who vigorously promoted the independence of his institution, was reported to be nervous of this interpretation. Whatever the reasoning, an initial plan to have the logos of the two universities adjacent in the centre of the bridge was replaced by a layout where each was attached to the side wall of the end of the bridge closest to its own side of the road.

It was clear to any observer that the School was being held back by its dated, often shabby and dispersed physical estate. Post-merger, beginning in 2007 during the early phases of the Directorship of Mike Luger, a case had been made for a new building to replace an outdated design and address long-term maintenance issues. Hotel facilities and executive education space were particularly poor. In the context of a large MBS operating deficit at that time, University President and Vice-Chancellor Alan Gilbert and Board of Governors Chair Norman Askew responded that the project would be supported if 'the School got its financial house in order and eliminated its deficit' and it could produce a building plan that did not require any cash (or loans). A competitive dialogue procurement process was launched in November 2007 to seek a development partner. Bruntwood, a leading local property firm, was confirmed as contractor in February 2011. With the School back in surplus, a clear plan had emerged with a detailed specification and business case.

The first phase of the redevelopment was the construction with development partner Bruntwood of a nineteen-storey hotel and an adjoining Executive Education Centre. A deal was struck with a hotel partner whereby the University contributed the land and a guaranteed number of bed nights in the hotel in return for the partner undertaking this part of the construction. Bruntwood developed the retail element of the programme on a long lease and took the rent from the shops and catering establishments. The main project was a bold transformation of the Precinct Centre which, despite the complexities involved, was more economical than a complete new build. Sustainability benefits were a by-product of this approach as the concrete frame and upper storeys were sound enough for reuse. During construction there was an iconic event in August 2015 when the Precinct bridge over Oxford Road was demolished, allowing the glazed Hive space to become the School's frontage to Oxford Road, with retail and catering units underneath and along the East side of the building facing a new park, University Green. The entrance is now via a large, glazed atrium opposite the hotel, leading up a wide staircase to a large concourse forming the spine of the School (Plate 7).

The financial picture was that in 2015 the University Board of Governors approved expenditure of £71.8m for the redevelopment of the Booth Street West site. This included a landmark donation from the Alliance family and was boosted by the securing of £9.7m from the UK Research Partnership Investment fund to enhance the research aspects of the building, including a state-of-the-art Data Analytics Visualisation Lab. During the life of the project construction cost had risen from an expected £43m in 2013 to £60m, and the final out-turn cost for the University once add-ons were included was £105m. To quote the Director of Estates and Services, Diana Hampson, 'The large increase in costs came as more information was found about the business school building and the impact on its refurbishment. Large amounts of unrecorded asbestos were discovered and the building was in some parts not constructed as shown in the available historic drawings.'[25] On the plus side, the maintenance would have been needed in any case and a transformative increase in quantity and quality of space was achieved.

The building also incorporated spaces named for key supporters, including the striking Eddie Davies Library after the Bolton-born businessman and philanthropist who was Chair of the Alliance MBS Advisory Board from 2013 until his untimely death in 2018. The highly successful Masood Entrepreneurship Centre, responsible for student entrepreneurship training across the University honours support from the brothers Tariq and Amer Masood.

For the first time in its existence AMBS premises were fit for an international business school, but the benefits were not only external. Staff and students had been even more dispersed during the decant for construction, occupying seven separate buildings around the campus. Coming together in the new building was, according to then Director Fiona Devine, a watershed moment in forging a common identity and weakening the pre-merger affiliations which appeared to have persisted for longer in AMBS than elsewhere in the University.[26]

Under the new leadership of Ken McPhail, following the promotion of Fiona Devine to be Dean and Vice-President of the Faculty of Humanities, AMBS is in a position which would surely meet and exceed the hopes and expectations of its founders sixty years ago as a world-class, research-intensive, full-service business school, the country's largest, engaged deeply with its city region and with a global reach and reputation.

Acknowledgements

The author extends grateful thanks to Jim Pendrill, Cary Cooper, Janine Ellis, Martin Walker, Fiona Devine, Diana Hampson, Andy Dyson, Rod Coombs, Jill Rubery, Nancy Rothwell and the John Rylands University Library Archive for sharing reminiscences and material about the history of the School.

Notes

1. Technically, it was not a merger as such but the double dissolution of VUM and UMIST and the foundation of the new University of Manchester, but it is commonly referred to as 'the merger', a convention followed here.
2. S. P. Keeble (1992) *The Ability to Manage: Study of British Management, 1890–1990*, Manchester: Manchester University Press, pp. 104–6.
3. Keeble (1992); E. S. Byng (1942) 'Post-entry training for administration from the industrial aspect', *Public Administration*, 21(1): 1–12.
4. H. M. V. (1920) 'Review: *Industrial Administration, a series of lectures*, Manchester: The University Press; New York: Longmans, Green & Co.', Nature, 106 (16 September), 74–75, p. 203.
5. Interview with Professor Sir Cary Cooper, 2025.
6. S. Caulkin (2003) Obituary: 'Reg Revans: Inspired management thinker of "action learning"', *Guardian*, 8 March, www.theguardian.com/news/2003/mar/08/guardianobituaries.simoncaulkin (accessed 21 February 2025).
7. The Faculty's name was changed when its remit was expanded to include the former Faculties of Education and of Law.
8. J. F. Wilson (1992) *The Manchester Experiment – A History of Manchester Business School 1965–1990*, London: Paul Chapman Publishing.
9. Wilson (1992: 20–21).
10. MANSMAN was the term used by B. Pullan and M. Abendstern (2000) *A History of the University of Manchester, 1951–73*, Manchester and New York: Manchester University Press, who described the School as a supra-departmental structure designed to coordinate activities also with the Faculty of Technology, p. 124.

11 Committee on Higher Education (1963, 23 September), *Higher Education: Report of the Committee appointed by the Prime Minister under the Chairmanship of Lord Robbins 1961–63*, Cmnd. 2154, London: HMSO. Another recommendation from the Robbins report had an unforeseen resonance for Manchester in 2024. It contained an unadopted recommendation for three Special Institutions for Scientific Education and Research (SISTERs) to be created, modelled on institutions such as the Massachusetts Institute of Technology. The Manchester College of Science Technology (latterly UMIST) was the basis for one of these. The name SISTER has been revived for the innovation district joint-venture created from the vacated UMIST campus.
12 Franks Report (1963) *British Business Schools*, London: British Institute of Management.
13 Pullan and Abendstern (2000: 124).
14 Wilson (1992: 22).
15 Lord Normanbrook (1964) *Report of a Working Party to the President of the FBI*, Federation of British Industries.
16 Despite the wishes of at least one incumbent, the US-style title of Dean has not been used to describe the leader of the business school in Manchester. For much of the sixty years the title of Director has been used but the most recent leaders have reverted to the standard University of Manchester terminology of Head of School.
17 T. Rickards (2016) *The Manchester Method Matters*, Self-published, Kindle Unlimited, ebook.
18 A more detailed account of the 'merger' of VUM and UMIST and subsequent developments can be found in L. Georghiou, 'Merger, global ambition and a renewed civic role – the University of Manchester from 2004 to 2024', in S. Jones (ed.) (2024) *Manchester Minds – A University History of Ideas*, Manchester: Manchester University Press.
19 A working party, independently chaired by Dr John Beacham, a regionally respected figure formerly of ICI (Imperial Chemical Industries) was mandated by the two Universities 'to consider various ways to develop a closer relationship'.
20 Pullan and Abendstern (2000: 136–37).
21 Some research staff in CRIC elected to join the new School of Social Sciences, an arrangement which persisted until the ESRC funding expired. Several had in the meantime gained substantial academic positions in MBS or Social Sciences.
22 Rickards (2016: 73–76).
23 Pullan and Abendstern (2000: 125).
24 R. Wilson (2019) 'BDP's refurbishment of the Alliance Manchester Business School', *Architects' Journal*, 17 May, www.architectsjournal.co.uk/buildings/bdps-refurbishment-of-the-alliance-manchester-business-school (accessed 21 February 2025).
25 Personal communication, March 2025.
26 Interview with Professor Fiona Devine, 18 February 2025.

ABBREVIATIONS

AI	artificial intelligence
AMBS	Alliance Manchester Business School
CRIC	Centre for Innovation and Competition
FESS	Faculty of Economic and Social Studies
GVC	global value chain
MBS	Manchester Business School
MIoIR	Manchester Institute of Innovation Research
MSM	Manchester School of Management
OECD	Organisation for Economic Co-operation and Development
PREST	Policy Research in Engineering Science and Technology
R&D	Research and Development
RAE	Research Assessment Exercise
SMEs	small and medium enterprises
UMIST	University of Manchester Institute of Science and Technology
UoM	University of Manchester
VUM	Victoria University Manchester

INTRODUCTION: THE ROLE OF BUSINESS SCHOOLS IN UNIVERSITIES, THE ECONOMY AND SOCIETY

Duncan Ivison and Ken McPhail

Whether it's dealing with economic disparities, global geopolitical upheaval, climate change or the impact of new technologies, we are living in pivotal times and the cumulative impact of these issues on the education sector has also been huge. As well as teaching the leaders of tomorrow, business schools have a crucial role to play in research discovery, promoting innovation and understanding how to tackle these grand challenges with impact alongside business.

Global disruption and the need to think differently about business and management

We are living through a period of profound disruption not experienced since the Industrial Revolution. The existential impacts of climate change and artificial intelligence, along with seismic shifts in the technological, societal, economic and geopolitical landscape, demand that we re-evaluate our established understanding of democracy and the economy. Any honest assessment of our existing political and economic models will conclude that at best the assumptions on which they are based no longer apply, and at worst that they have contributed to the challenges we now face. If that is the case, then what we desperately need from business schools and universities is not more of the same 'internationally excellent' research about business and management. We need to fundamentally reimagine how economic activity can be truly shaped as a force for good.

Reimagining business and education

At the same time our understanding of the role of universities in society, and the business models on which they are based, are also fundamentally changing. Universities are being reimagined as sources of social and technological innovation and entrepreneurship that will drive socio-technological transition, while also generating regional economic growth. The reimagination of business and management and the reimagination of universities are symbiotic.

Of course, at the heart of both universities and business schools are students and learners, the most powerful agents in responding to the challenges we face. Yet we also need to reimagine their potential as collaborators and partners rather than just as repositories for our knowledge. It is also essential that universities and business schools think differently about how they teach business and management students so that they are equipped with the necessary skills to embrace this new world and have a positive impact upon it.

Huge change

Profound changes, accelerated by the COVID-19 pandemic, are reshaping the world of work and employment, increasing the diversity of workplaces and reshaping the distinction between formal and informal work sectors. These are just some of the changes that demand that business schools and universities think and engage with communities in more direct and engaged ways. It is our firm belief that the great universities of the future will be those that can accelerate the time between discovery and impact, whatever the academic discipline. To do that they will have to work in partnership with business, governments, communities and other non-governmental organisations.

As a leading research-intensive university, ranked among the best in the world, the University of Manchester naturally has the capacity to carry out world-leading research. But increasingly we realise this is not enough. Yes, we need ground-breaking fundamental research, but we also need to translate this research into societal impact. And we won't do this only by publishing in world-leading academic journals.

Indeed, Manchester is a powerful example of a university that sits cheek by jowl with communities which have not benefited enough from economic growth. Although the centre of the city has witnessed an economic transformation since the mid-1990s, large parts of the city region remain blighted by social and economic deprivation. Our University and Business School need to be part of the solution to these significant and ongoing challenges.

Our civic responsibility

Indeed, universities have a unique capacity to bring people together across divides and help rebuild trust in civil institutions. For example, in 2024 the University convened a group of community leaders and academic experts from across Greater Manchester to explore the causes and aftermath of the race riots seen across Britain in summer 2024.

As one of the participants at that event put it, we need to 'ask the hard questions to have the hard conversations'. We cannot think of a better way to capture the role of universities in providing a forum for dialogue. Today, social media is often blamed for fuelling tensions, but participants in our workshop noted that the use of misinformation predates the internet. More importantly, rancour on social media seems to be more a symptom than a cause. The deeper problem is growing mistrust in the core institutions of liberal democracies – the judiciary, media, government and universities.[1]

Moral questions

This leads to a wider and deeper debate about the true role of universities in terms of debate, discovery and teaching. We ask the question here because many of the answers to the grand societal challenges that we face are also creating moral issues too, and it's vital that business leaders operate in an environment grounded in a strong moral framework.

This matters, because there is a wider expectation from society and consumers today that businesses (and their supply chains) abide by a clear moral framework. It also matters because relentless economic liberalisation and globalisation have undermined the communal structures within which people find support and common cause, leaving a significant proportion of societies in the West socially and culturally disoriented.

At the same time, large-scale immigration has generated economic and cultural unease and resentment in large segments of the population. Economic and trade policy, cultural liberalisation, mass migration, along with rising nationalism, have created fertile ground for reactive political forces to thrive. Citizens feel disempowered by globalisation and this fuels populist reactions.

Value-informed approach

This means that at the organisational level business schools and universities need to think about their disciplines in the context of a greater 'ethical whole', because this is what communities expect from their leaders – whether in politics, education or business. Success for universities in the future will be tied to the ability to navigate this environment and deal with growing levels of mistrust in liberal democracies. But success will also require giving students the principles and skills they need to keep learning (and acting) in the right way.

Universities must be convenors of dialogue, rather than direct political participants in it. They need to take a *value-informed* approach to their convening power and responsibility, with academic freedom, social responsibility and truth-seeking at its core. This is particularly relevant for civic universities, as anchor institutions in their cities, owing to their distinctive capacity to bring people together and foster deeper understanding between interest groups, while serving as trusted partners for local communities and – at the same time – aspiring to global relevance and impact.

Indeed, a university's 'North Star' must be academic freedom, diversity of opinion and inclusion, and these are far more dependent on each other than in opposition. Freedom is needed to get to the truth, but you will not get the best answers unless you have sufficiently diverse opinions around the table.

Reimagining business as a force for good

Informed debate and new research breakthroughs need to be followed up by changes to the way we do business and generate new kinds of value. Indeed, there is recognition that business and management may be one of our best hopes for finding solutions to many of the grand challenges we face.

For some time, societal, governmental and investor expectations about the purpose of business have been shifting away from the view that the sole purpose of business is to generate profits for shareholders. Business is now expected to be a force for good, generating value in different ways and for different groups. For instance, there is a growing recognition of the extent to which those from poorer backgrounds, along with women and other minoritised groups, have been disadvantaged by our business systems.[2] This recognition has come alongside calls for more equitable employment opportunities, career progression and pay.

Being a force for good requires the exploration of new roles for business that create economic, political and social value. It involves developing a different understanding of corporate purpose, grounded in addressing societal problems profitably and harnessing the role of grand challenges as a source of innovation and value generation. The central question is: what needs to be reimagined, and specifically how can business serve the collective interest rather than the individual interest?

Given the scale and urgency of the grand challenges, there is a need to accelerate our reimagining of business as a force for good.[3] And a need to increase our understanding of the interdependencies between them (e.g. between environmental and societal challenges) and whether a just transition to new forms of production/consumption systems is possible.[4]

The power of corporations

The debate around reimagining business and the wider capitalist model, and one of the reasons why this is such a pressing debate, is that it comes at a time when large corporations now exercise the type of public power historically associated with governments. Indeed, many companies are now far more valuable than some nation-states. As both Davis and Mayer state, the decisions of corporate management and the practices of business now have at least a commensurate, if not greater, impact on the lives of individuals for good and bad, than the actions of government.[5]

This means that the negative impacts of 'big business' have the potential to become a systemic threat. However, the paradox is that a populist response might be to argue that the problem is the size of the state and excessive regulation, and that an even more laissez-faire approach is needed. Of course, states are still hugely influential. As we write, escalating tariff and trade wars reflect the political pressure to protect local jobs. In trying to rebut this populist standpoint and reimagine business, perhaps the biggest challenge is the difficulty in agreeing what we mean by promoting business as a force for good. What does 'good' look like? For instance, does it mean good jobs for people in your own workforce, or is it more about good jobs in your supply chains?

Focus on process

The question is complicated. We should, however, focus more on *processes*. This is where reimagining business schools comes in, and the need to find manageable ways of navigating this complexity, because the global challenges we face demand a new way of thinking about business decision making, organisational structures and governance structures.

At the same time, we need to be asking who gets to decide what actions will be taken. Who gets a voice in decision making? How do workers and other rights holders get involved in processes that impact on them? How do you democratise business?

In recent years, efforts have been made to tackle some of these questions in specific industries. For instance, in the wake of the Rana Plaza disaster in Bangladesh in 2013 (in which more than 1,000 people died when a garments factory collapsed), Western companies which produce clothing in the country have signed up to various new accords and agreements, an example of where businesses providing soft regulatory mechanisms could be part of the answer.

Indeed, one of the most radical reimaginations of the role of business in society has been the United Nations Guiding Principles on Business and Human Rights (UNGP), which were created in 2011. Based on the fundamental principles of *'protect, respect, remedy'*, the principles reimagine a role for business in both promoting the most basic needs required for human flourishing as well as providing access to justice where those needs are violated.[6] What began as an attempt to reimagine a role for business in protecting human rights has now been incorporated into international standards.

Being a force for good requires the exploration of new roles for business that create economic, political and social value. It involves developing a different understanding of corporate *purpose*, grounded in addressing societal problems profitably and harnessing the role of grand challenges as a source of innovation and value generation. However, it also involves reconceptualising the relationship between business and the state and experience of work. The focus on solving societal problems should not be divorced from the experience of work and practice of management. There are several examples of radical attempts to reimagine the purpose of business in society, like the UNGP. Yet, while these imaginations can act as a powerful bridge between convention and transformation, we also need to foster a clearer understanding of the relationship between imagination and innovation, the role of collaboration and the impact of national regulation.

Reimagining business schools

Some would argue that business schools are ideally placed to take up the challenge of reimagining business as a force for good in ways that inform practice and policy. Others might go further and say that if business schools are not at the heart of reimagining business, they may lose their legitimacy and cease to have a reason to exist at all. If the purpose of business needs to be reimagined, business schools will need to change in order to be a major catalyst in this process. As we write, calls for a more purpose-driven, transformational response from business schools are gaining traction.

In their recent paper, McPhail, Kafouros, McKiernan and Cornelius called for a fundamental recasting of the roots of the modern pedagogic process to refocus on education, bringing back contemplation, deliberation and character formation, and shifting schools away from training centres to be recognisable builders of society.[7] They make the case that the way business schools have taught students to think about business, along with business and management scholarship, may have become so fixed that our short-term interests have trumped those of future generations.

The question comes back to how we *structure* business schools in ways that helps address grand challenges. How do we ensure that business schools are at the forefront of policy debates, and ensure groups of academics work together across disciplines to propose concrete policy actions? In Chapter 9, these are precisely the themes that Gerard P Hodgkinson and Elvira Uyarra explore, as they discuss the need for academics to work far more collaboratively across disciplines to make stronger policy impact and tackle grand challenges.

At Alliance Manchester Business School, the largest business school in the UK, these questions are particularly pertinent because we have the resources to reimagine business teaching in ground-breaking ways. The question we must ask ourselves is: what barriers and institutional structures are stopping us from utilising these resources to the full?

Building on strengths

For Alliance Manchester Business School, being embedded within both the University of Manchester and the city of Manchester may be our biggest advantage when it comes to reimagining business as a force for good. Its position within the University is also a massive strength for the business school when it comes to promoting interdisciplinary work. And its position within the city's burgeoning innovation ecosystem provides the infrastructure to translate new business ideas into viable businesses (see Chapter 2).

Indeed, we need to be as entrepreneurial and innovative as we possibly can to respond to the huge technological changes taking place around us. We also need to be innovative in our collaborations, and embrace the current UK Government's focus on growth, innovation and entrepreneurship.

Building new and creative partnerships will be key to addressing global challenges. And those partnerships extend to students in terms of being given repeated opportunities to put theory into practice by going out into the field. Crucially, they then need to bring those learnings back into the classroom. We also need to find new ways of working, new structures, and new ways of teaching and learning that reflect the world we live in and help students embrace the entrepreneurial mindset that is needed to address societal challenges, all the while reflecting the diversity of our community which will be key to identifying solutions.

These debates are all most timely given that the University of Manchester is, as we write, working on a collective vision for the next decade. Built on our strong foundations of excellent teaching and world-class research, the university's vision sets out to create an outstanding experience for both students and staff, and one that is both deeply rooted in Manchester and globally significant.

Book structure

Our first three chapters explore grand challenges, economic growth and the purpose of business in more depth. In the first, Frank Geels and Sacha Sadan discuss how we navigate the net zero transition, while in the second, Lou Cordwell looks at catalysing Manchester's innovation ecosystem to unlock economic growth. In chapter 3, Sir Terry Leahy and Philip McCann look at the challenges posed by regional inequalities across the UK.

The next five chapters explore the themes of creativity, technology and meaningful work. In Chapter 4 Catherine Mann and Markos Zachariadis discuss the future of money and finance, while in the following chapter Sir Cary Cooper and Tera Ellas look at the importance of management and leadership in terms of promoting better wellbeing and productivity in the workplace. Jill Rubery and Andrew Westwood then explore how business schools can contribute to a more inclusive society for all workers, while in the following chapter Michelle Carter and Richard Allmendinger ask whether we should shape the future of artificial intelligence (AI) or whether AI will shape us. In Chapter 8 there is an exploration of the 'creativity crisis' in business schools by Bruce Tether and John McAuliffe.

The final three chapters look at the broad themes of knowledge, ethics and politics. In Chapter 9 Gerard P Hodgkinson and Elvira Uyarra discuss the future of business and management knowledge. This is then followed by a look at the impact of geopolitical tensions on the future of the multinational and how business schools need to respond to global uncertainty, written by Peter Buckley and Axèle Giroud.

Our final chapter, by Fiona Devine and Nazir Afzal – 'A Business School for the Twenty-First Century' – looks at the pressure being put on the ideal of universities as places of dialogue and truth-seeking, and the importance of remembering how to disagree well and engage in a genuine conversation and debate, as opposed to merely restating our untested beliefs.

Notes

1. D. Ivison (2024) '*Introduction: The "vicissitudes of liberalism"*', in D. Ivison (ed.) *Research Handbook on Liberalism*, Elgaronline, https://doi.org/10.4337/9781839109034.00006
2. K. W. Crenshaw (2017) *On Intersectionality: Essential Writings*, New York: New Press.
3. A. A. Gümüsay and J. Reinecke (2022) 'Researching for desirable futures: from real utopias to imagining alternatives', *Journal of Management Studies*, 59: 236–42.
4. X. Wang and K. Lo (2021) 'Just transition: a conceptual review', *Energy Research & Social Science*, 82: 102291.
5. C. Mayer (2020) 'The future of the corporation and the economics of purpose', *Journal of Management Studies*, 58(3): 887–901; G. Davis (2020) 'Corporate purpose needs democracy', *Journal of Management Studies*, 58(3): 902–13.
6. K. McPhail and C. A. Adams (2016) 'Corporate respect for human rights: meaning, scope, and the shifting order of discourse', *Accounting, Auditing and Accountability Journal*, 29: 650–78; J. G. Ruggie (2018) 'Multinationals as global institution: power, authority and relative autonomy', *Regulation & Governance*, 12: 317–33; J. G. Ruggie, C. Rees and R. Davis (2021) 'Ten years after: from UN Guiding Principles to multi-fiduciary obligations', *Business and Human Rights Journal*, 6: 179–97.
7. This introductory chapter draws heavily on the article by K. McPhail, M. Kafouros, P. McKiernan and N. Cornelius (2024) 'Reimagining business and management as a force for good', *British Journal of Management*, 35(3): 1099–112.

1
NAVIGATING THE NET ZERO TRANSITION

Frank W. Geels and Sacha Sadan

Introduction

As events across the world remind us daily, climate change is a grand societal challenge that will affect many aspects of societies and economies through the impact of droughts, floods, crop failures, fires, sea level rises and heat stress. In response to the challenge, since 2019 more than 140 countries have set net zero targets covering 88 per cent of global emissions.[1] Many non-governmental actors such as individual firms and cities have also announced their own net zero targets.

Yet, meeting goals to tackle climate change will require drastic reductions in greenhouse gas (GHG) emissions which, as the Intergovernmental Panel on Climate Change (IPCC) says, can only be achieved through 'rapid and far-reaching transitions in energy, land, urban and infrastructure (including transport and buildings), and industrial systems'.[2] However, at the time of writing this chapter, these challenges have arguably been made even greater by the 'drill, baby drill' mantra of the current US presidency, and the associated weakening of electric vehicle (EV) and renewable energy support policies and the scuppering of climate change science.

Huge structural change

Net zero transitions will involve huge structural change processes in the main GHG-emitting systems such as energy production (which accounted for 36 per cent of global GHG emissions in 2021), heavy industry (21 per cent), agriculture/forestry/other land uses (18 per cent), transport (14 per cent), buildings (6 per cent) and waste (4 per cent).[3] Net zero transitions in these systems will require shifts to new technologies (such as solar-photovoltaic [PV] modules, wind turbines, electric vehicles, heat pumps, electric arc furnaces, home insulation, agroecology, plant-based meat and dairy products), new production processes (e.g. battery plants, green steel manufacturing) and new infrastructures (e.g. battery-charging facilities, electricity grid reinforcements and extensions). It will also demand new consumption and behavioural patterns (e.g. meat-free diets, purchasing green electricity), new government policies (e.g. adoption subsidies, capital grants, green standards and regulations), new supply chains (e.g. for components, materials and minerals), new public perceptions (e.g. of alternative meat products or cars) and new financial investments.

What is interesting is that until recently net zero transitions were predominantly understood in terms of additional costs, assuming that decarbonisation would have negative effects on national economic growth or company profitability. In recent years, however, the debate has changed, with a far greater emphasis on economic opportunities and productivity improvements. For instance, the International Monetary Fund's (IMF) *World Economic Outlook* suggests that 'decarbonization policies focused on innovation policy (such as research subsidies) could trigger waves of technological change that would boost productivity and growth in the medium to long term'.[4] And a UK Treasury report similarly concluded: 'The transition to net zero will create new opportunities for economic growth and job creation across the country. The demand for low-carbon goods and services will encourage new industries to emerge, with the potential to boost investment levels and productivity growth.'[5]

One reason for this change in mindset is that the increasing deployment and diffusion of wind turbines, solar-PV modules and EVs has been accompanied by steep cost reductions which have made renewable electricity technologies the cheapest electricity-generation options in most parts of the world.[6] Another reason is that the increasing diffusion of solar-PV, wind turbines and EVs has led to a global innovation race in which the US and Europe aim to catch up with China, which dominates the global manufacturing of many low-carbon technologies.[7] In 2022 the then US administration also introduced the Inflation Reduction Act, which boosted domestic manufacturing and deployment of clean energy technologies with $369 billion in subsidies, a transformative amount of money. In response, the European Commission introduced the 2023 Net Zero Industry Act, with similar ambitions.

Transition plans

Cost reductions, market-creating subsidies and the perception of economic opportunities have also led to increasing engagement and investment from companies, many of whom are reorienting their strategies in low-carbon directions and/or creating transition plans.[8] Nevertheless, firms and other actors may be cautious or even reluctant to seriously commit to net zero transitions, especially when upfront costs are high, future benefits are uncertain or diverse transition pathways create uncertainties about which one to choose. While plans and strategies are important, net zero transitions need to be navigated, which involves processes like learning-by-doing, collaboration and negotiation.[9] In this chapter we not only look at how businesses can navigate this accelerating transition but also explore the role that finance has to play in making sure companies meet their net zero commitments, and the fact that climate change is a financially material issue that needs to be reported on by businesses. We conclude with a discussion around what this also means for business school teaching and research.

Challenges

These huge debates create challenges. For instance, some business leaders still see net zero targets as simply too far away on the horizon. In some industries there is no cohesive plan in terms of how net zero targets can be achieved. And for many companies net zero is difficult to implement and costs money. But the huge increase in transition capital now available can provide tangible support. Here, the UK has a particularly strong opportunity, given that it has a large and thriving financial services industry. The injection of transition capital presents significant opportunities for long-term investment in the economy, aligning with the current government's specific focus on growth. Companies need to evolve their business models and ethos in response to climate change. Assessing the environmental damage they are causing, determining the associated costs, calculating the impact on future

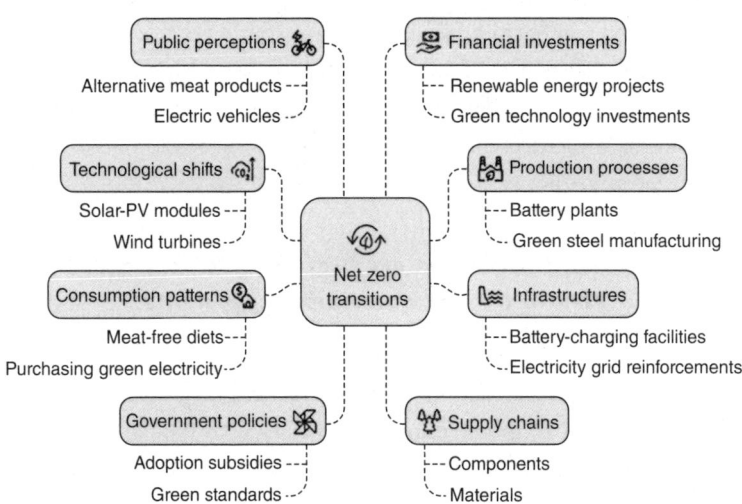

Figure 1.1 Structural changes for net zero transitions. Chart supported by NapkinAI, March 2025.

profits and identifying the necessary changes to mitigate this are all part of the equation too.

Accelerating net zero transitions – the evidence

It is worth first outlining here how the net zero transition has not just started from scratch but has been in the making since the 2000s. There are four overwhelming pieces of evidence which support the claim that the transition is accelerating.

CO_2 emissions in Europe, the US and other high-income countries have started to decrease since the late 2000s

As the chart in Figure 1.2 shows, emissions are falling in Europe, the US and many other high-income countries. This is mostly because of increases in renewable electricity, some degree of industrial offshoring (i.e. relocation to other countries) and a shift from coal to gas (especially in the US). Meanwhile China, which as the largest CO_2 emitting country accounted for 31 per cent of global CO_2 emissions in 2022, appears to be approaching 'peak emissions', partly because of increases in renewable electricity.[10] Although *global* emissions have continued to increase (because of understandable development ambitions in emerging economies), these decreasing emissions in several world regions offer some reason for hope.

Low-carbon transitions are beginning to accelerate in electricity and automobility systems

The percentage of renewables in electricity generation has rapidly increased since 2011, reaching 35.2 per cent in Europe (in 2022), 22.7 per cent in the US (in 2023) and 30.7 per cent in China (in 2023).[11] Renewable electricity shares grew particularly rapidly in Germany and the UK, expanding from low levels in the 1990s to reach 52.4 per cent and 46.0 per cent, respectively in 2023 (Figure 1.3).

Although Europe leads this transition in renewable electricity shares (in terms of percentages), China leads in the absolute deployment of

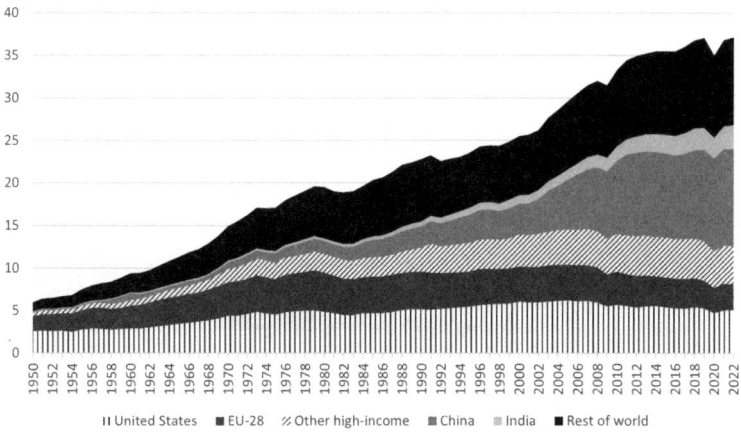

Figure 1.2 Annual global CO2 emissions (in billion tonnes) per region, 1950–2022. Constructed using data from Our World in Data, *CO₂ and Greenhouse Gas Emissions Data Explorer*, https://ourworldindata.org/explorers/co2 (accessed 6 May 2025).

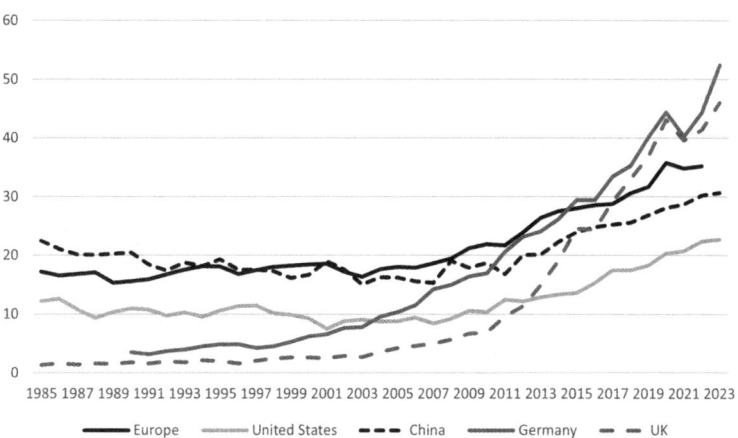

Figure 1.3 Share of electricity production from renewables (in percentages) in Europe, the US, China, Germany and the UK, 1985–2023. Constructed using data from Our World in Data, *Renewable Energy*, https://ourworldindata.org/renewable-energy (accessed 6 May 2025).

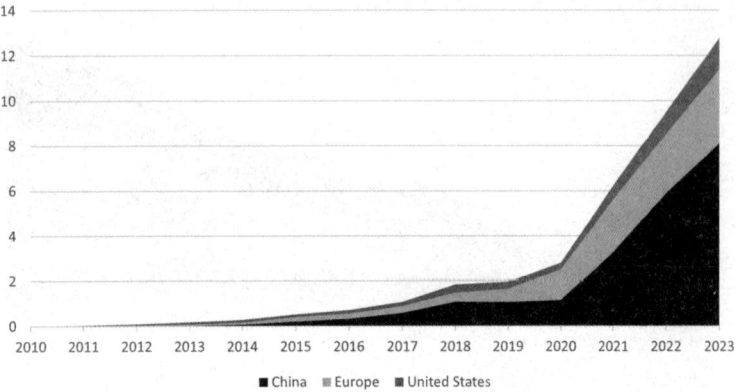

Figure 1.4 Annual domestic sales of EVs (in millions) in China, Europe and the US, 2010–23. Constructed using data from IEA (2024) *Global EV Outlook 2024: Moving Towards Increased Affordability*, Paris: International Energy Agency.

solar-PV and wind energy, enabling it to benefit from economies of scale and learning-by-doing processes. China also leads in the domestic sales and deployment of EVs (which include battery EVs [BEVs] and plug-in hybrid electric vehicles), both in absolute sales and as a percentage of all passenger car sales (Figure 1.4). In 2023, BEV market share sales reached 38 per cent in China, 21 per cent in Europe and 9.5 per cent in the US (Figure 1.5).[12] Global EV sales reached 18 per cent of all new car sales in 2023, up from less than 5 per cent in 2020, suggesting a rapid transition is underway.

Other systems are still lagging behind electricity and automobility. But because of the lessons from electricity and automobility there is now more hope than in the mid-2010s that low-carbon transitions in these other systems can also accelerate in the coming years.

Increasing deployment has significantly reduced costs because of scale economies in production, learning-by-doing and ongoing technical innovations

Between 2010 and 2022, the cost of electricity decreased by 89 per cent for solar-PV, by 69 per cent for onshore wind and by 59 per cent

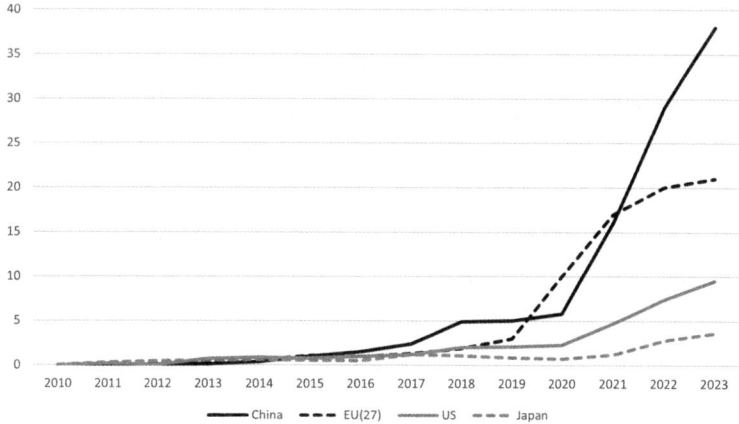

Figure 1.5 Annual domestic sales of BEVs as percentage of market share in China, Europe and the US, 2010–23. Constructed using data from IEA (2024) *Global EV Outlook 2024: Moving Towards Increased Affordability*, Paris: International Energy Agency.

for offshore wind (see Figure 1.6). The price of lithium-ion battery packs, which are the most expensive component of electric vehicles, also fell significantly (by 88 per cent) between 2010 and 2022, leading to the expectation that EVs will become cheaper to buy than petrol or diesel cars by 2026/27.[13]

Investment into low-carbon technologies globally has increased 50-fold in the past two decades

The final piece of evidence relates to the huge investment in low-carbon technologies since the turn of the century. Over the course of two decades it has increased from $33 billion in 2004 to $1.77 trillion in 2023.[14] These investments, which enable firms and other actors to develop and deploy low carbon innovations, have mostly gone to renewable energy (solar-PV, wind) and EVs, although investments in power grids, heat pumps, clean industry and energy storage have also started to increase.

The world is thus beginning to gear up to mobilise large amounts of money for climate mitigation, although there is quite some way to

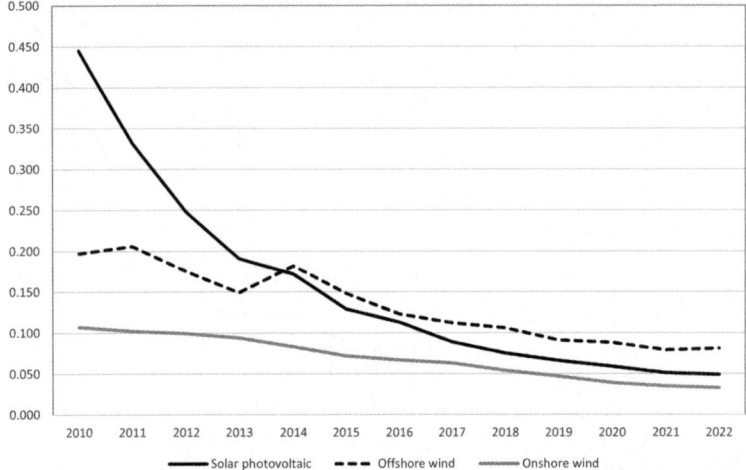

Figure 1.6 Global weighted average levelised cost of electricity for solar-PV, offshore wind and onshore wind, 2010–22, in 2022 US$/kWh. Constructed using data from IRENA (2023) *Renewable Power Generation Costs in 2022*, Abu Dhabi: International Renewable Energy Agency.

go. Estimates suggest that global net zero transitions require between USD 3 and 3.5 trillion in additional annual investments until 2050.[15]

Transition plans

What is clear is that innovation processes are a driving force behind this accelerating transition. Finance is flowing into green energy because investors and companies see the commercial opportunities. At the same time industrial policy, such as through capital grants, loans and other incentives which reduce the risk of investment, is also having a major impact, as are market-creation policies (such as purchase subsidies and regulations). As technologies become cheaper and more competitive, so market demand grows and finance flows increase, in turn further boosting innovation. In short, innovation, competition and market creation have unleashed a green innovation race in which companies want to, and have to, keep up and invest. For instance, what has happened in electricity and EVs has mostly been driven by policy incentives, innovation, deployment and competition.

Metrics

Metrics undoubtedly have a role to play in helping companies deal with and manage the transition. As such, reporting and disclosure are important because they help investors assess companies and price risks and opportunities. The low-carbon transition has implications for all elements of business, and the transition should be seen as a cross-cutting challenge for organisations that demands major change in processes and structures.

To this end, recent years have seen much work around building a set of clearly defined sustainability metrics to guide companies. In particular, here in the UK the Financial Conduct Authority (FCA) has implemented in its rulebook the Task Force on Climate-Related Financial Disclosures (TCFD), which has been developing a framework to help public companies and other organisations disclose climate-related risks. In the wake of COP26, the UK Treasury set up a Transition Plan Taskforce (TPT) with the FCA closely involved both at the strategic and technical levels. This brought together government, regulators, corporates, asset owners, accounting bodies and civil society behind this agenda. This broad church was deliberate because it was clear there was a need for a united voice.

Transition plans done well – those which are robust, credible and disclosed – may alleviate, rather than create, legal risks faced by companies. Such plans allow them to communicate their targets and actions today, recognising that they are dependent on external factors outside of their control, such that their plans will need to adapt and evolve over time. The important thing is that statements are made on the basis that companies have the will and means to achieve them, and are made on a best-efforts basis. Today, many FTSE 100 companies are voluntarily disclosing transition plans and there is a growing regulatory focus on transition plan disclosure. But this isn't just about the largest listed companies. It is also essential that private companies take on board best practice too, such as collaborating on innovative solutions with industry peers, non-governmental organisations and government officials.

Challenges

It is understandable that initial transition plans may fall short, as companies face the pressure of meeting net zero targets (especially from investors who want to price the future) without possessing all the necessary knowledge or solutions. This is precisely why innovation, exploration and learning are so essential.

Transition plans also pose specific challenges around assurance because auditors are trained to develop clear and precise answers. Much work is going on globally with auditors, but this is a rolling, evolving process, and to an extent companies are going to have to 'get comfortable being uncomfortable'. Indeed, if one factors in Scope 3 emissions – those which occur indirectly in an organisation's value chain and are not produced by the organisation itself – then it is inevitable that most businesses will also need to work across borders to find solutions, which makes the challenge even more problematic. Speaking the same sustainability language poses a huge challenge.

The UK is, however, well positioned to be at the forefront of this global assurance drive. It has a very strong financial market (its bond market will become particularly important in terms of funding the transition), an established rule of law and a track record of demonstrating international leadership on key regulatory issues, while continuing to collaborate effectively in relevant international forums. For instance, the FCA has also been working closely with the International Sustainability Standards Board (ISSB) and its mission to create a common, global language for companies around the world to communicate their sustainability stories in a consistent and comparable way. The ISSB's first sustainability-related reporting standards – IFRS S1 and S2 – answer the clear market demand for complete, consistent, comparable and reliable corporate sustainability disclosures. The ISSB has also assumed responsibility for UK TPT disclosure materials in a bid to streamline and consolidate frameworks, thereby allowing governments around the world to start building their own specific transition models based on the UK TPT.

This is all positive news, but there is still a way to go. Latest estimates suggest only around 60 per cent of the world's GDP is currently on track to use ISSB standards. In the meantime, there are also challenges around competing global transition plan frameworks, with the EU pushing its own set of more onerous standards, not withstanding ongoing efforts to reduce the burden via the Omnibus Directive. In the UK mandatory transition plans are being considered, while the Government is planning to consult on using future UK Sustainability Reporting Standards based on global ISSB standards.

Summary and key recommendations

Low-carbon transitions have become a top management consideration, affecting the long-term performance of firms. For instance, companies like automakers, electric utilities, steel companies, oil refineries, solar-PV and wind turbine manufacturers are increasingly caught up in a green global innovation race. Early movers may benefit, while failure to participate or catch up with Chinese companies – which are leading in many low-carbon technologies – may lead to financial losses and decline. German car companies, for example, which have long resisted and delayed low-carbon transitions, are now facing stiff competition from Chinese EVs which are eroding their market share and leading to plant closures.[16]

The wider picture here is that most companies want to be on the right side of the net zero debate and fully engage with it. They understand that to attract top talent now and in the future they must deliver on their promises with positive actions from the ground up, and that they need to show genuine commitment. Likewise, it is just as important that the world's biggest financiers and fund managers – as well as its biggest companies – sign up to and implement net zero commitments. It is essential that capital starts flowing not only to those companies that are rising to the net zero challenge, but also to those identifying financial opportunities for climate adaption.

Role of business schools

Against this backdrop business schools are well placed to help address the challenges around low-carbon transitions in various sectors and industries. But this requires business schools to understand low-carbon transitions as a cross-cutting challenge for organisations rather than as a specialised topic to be addressed by environmental, social and governance scholars. It also requires business schools to move beyond their divisional silos and develop broader synthetic research programmes that start with real-world problems rather than with specific theories (see Chapter 9). These programmes should aim to incorporate insights from subfields such as innovation studies, strategic management, international business, organisation studies, finance, marketing and public relations.

Role of auditing, accounting and finance

Every business – and business career – is being affected by the sustainability agenda and its impact will only grow further. Against this backdrop auditors and financial professionals will have a crucial role to play in terms of ensuring the right sustainability metrics are assessed within a specific business or organisation.

Business schools will have to speak the language of sustainability accounting, embedding the subject in curricula and ensuring students are equipped with the skill sets required to study and analyse transition plans – and have the necessary skills to tell the difference between good and poor ones.

As new valuation techniques and rankings are invented, so accounting and finance academics have a key role to play in helping the assurance industry to number-crunch the data and price climate risk and net zero ambitions accordingly. They can also assess what metrics are material and which ones can be ignored.

Notes

1. United Nations (2024) *For a Livable Climate: Net-zero Commitments Must Be Backed by Credible Action*, www.un.org/en/climatechange/net-zero-coalition (accessed 22 April 2024).
2. IPCC (2018) *Global Warming of 1.5°C: An IPCC Special Report on the Impacts of Global Warming of 1.5°C above Pre-industrial Levels and Related Global Greenhouse Gas Emission Pathways, in the Context of Strengthening the Global Response to the Threat of Climate Change, Sustainable Development, and Efforts to Eradicate Poverty; Summary for Policymakers*, www.ipcc.ch/sr15/, p. 21 (accessed 18 April 2025).
3. Global net anthropocentric GHG emissions (in gigatonnes of carbon dioxide equivalent) by sector in 2021, S. Boehm, L. Jeffery, J. Hecke, C. Schumer, J. Jaeger, C. Fyson, K. Levin, A. Nilsson, S. Naimoli, E. Daly, J. Thwaites, K. Lebling, R. Waite, J. Collis, M. Sims, N. Singh, E. Grier, W. Lamb, S. Castellanos, A. Lee, M. Geffray, R. Santo, M. Balehegn, M. Petroni and M. Masterson (2023) *State of Climate Action 2023*. Berlin and Cologne, San Francisco and Washington, DC: Bezos Earth Fund, Climate Action Tracker, Climate Analytics, ClimateWorks Foundation, NewClimate Institute, the United Nations Climate Change High-Level Champions, and World Resources Institute, p. 4, https://doi.org/10.46830/wrirpt.23.00010.
4. IMF (2020) *World Economic Outlook, October 2020: A Long and Difficult Ascent*, Washington, DC: International Monetary Fund, p. 88.
5. HM Treasury (2020) *Net Zero Review: Interim Report*, London: HM Treasury, p. 3.
6. IEA (2023a) *The Energy World Is Set to Change Significantly by 2030, Based on Today's Policy Settings Alone*, Paris: International Energy Agency, www.iea.org/news/the-energy-world-is-set-to-change-significantly-by-2030-based-on-today-s-policy-settings-alone (accessed 6 May 2025).
7. IEA (2023b) *The State of Clean Technology Manufacturing: An Energy Technology Perspectives Special Briefing, Paris:* International Energy Agency.
8. R. Bohnsack, A. Kolk, J. Pinkse and C. Bidmon (2020) 'Driving the electric bandwagon: the dynamics of incumbents' sustainable product innovation', *Business Strategy and the Environment*, 29(2): 727–43.
9. F. W. Geels (2024) *Advanced Introduction to Sustainability Transitions*, Cheltenham: Edward Elgar.
10. CarbonBrief (2024) *Analysis: Monthly Drop Hints that China's CO_2 Emissions May Have Peaked in 2023*, www.carbonbrief.org/analysis-monthly-drop-hints-that-chinas-co2-emissions-may-have-peaked-in-2023/ (accessed 6 May 2025).
11. Geels (2024).

12 IEA (2024) *Global EV Outlook 2024: Moving Towards Increased Affordability*, Paris: International Energy Agency.
13 IEA (2024).
14 BNEF (2024) *Energy Transition Investment Trends 2024 Tracking global investment in the low-carbon transition*, Bloomberg New Energy Finance.
15 McKinsey (2022) *The Net-Zero Transition: What It Would Cost, What It Could Bring*, New York: McKinsey Global Institute.
16 I. Richter and K. S. Stegen (2022) 'A choreography of delay: the response of German auto incumbents to environmental policy', *Environmental Innovation and Societal Transitions*, 45 (2022): 1–13.

2

CATALYSING MANCHESTER'S INNOVATION ECOSYSTEM TO UNLOCK ECONOMIC GROWTH

Lou Cordwell

Introduction

Innovation has been central to the mission of the University of Manchester (UoM) ever since it was established in 1824, and it continues to be just as critical today, with the University the largest innovation asset in Manchester. In fact, Britain's universities are extraordinary economic assets, internationally recognised for their world-class research, high-quality education and training and ability to attract talent and investment from around the globe. Research by London Economics for the Russell Group found that for every £1 of public funds invested in research at Russell Group institutions, more than £8.50 was generated for the UK economy.[1] Unlocking their full potential will be critical to creating a vibrant and future-focused innovation economy and in helping deliver the present Labour Government's ambitions for growth.

Founded to meet the economic needs of Manchester and the wider region, ground-breaking discoveries at UoM have sparked entirely new industries to an extent that can be asserted by only a handful of other leading UK universities – whether that's Rutherford splitting the atom and ushering in the nuclear age, Turing's pioneering work that laid the foundations of artificial intelligence (AI) or Geim and Novoselov's revolutionary science of graphene and two-dimensional materials. Today UoM is the UK's largest single-campus university, ranking thirty-fourth globally and fifth in the UK for research excellence.[2] It also holds the distinction of being ranked the second university, worldwide, for the impact of its activities in advancing the United Nations' Sustainable Development Goals.[3] Accounting for 93 per cent of public research and development (R&D) spend in Greater Manchester, UoM recognises that it has a lead role to play in creating a vibrant and future-focused innovation economy.

UoM's scale and excellence in research, innovation and skills development position it at the heart of the city's next growth phase, and also as a crucial delivery partner for the UK's modern Industrial Strategy in terms of ambitions around growing high-value clusters, creating high-value spin-outs and start-ups, supporting small and medium enterprises (SMEs) and scale-ups to adopt new technologies and skills, crowding in private investment in near-market R&D and attracting private sector investment to the UK.

UoM has specifically made catalysing growth for the region and the UK a strategic priority, and in October 2024 its President and Vice-Chancellor, Duncan Ivison, launched Unit M, a new innovation capability seed funded by the University, to lead this regional growth effort. With a mandate to accelerate industry access to our extensive innovation assets, capabilities and talent, Unit M will drive growth in start-ups and scale-ups, diffuse technologies into SMEs and attract foreign direct investment to the region and the UK.[4] Making it easier for partners to collaborate by opening up the University, Unit M will deploy the University's scale, research expertise and global network to attract new – and expand existing – innovation-intensive businesses to the region, enabling the University to be much more flexible and responsive to industry. At the heart of the Unit M mission is an ambition to pioneer a more inclusive, more sustainable model of growth – social innovation hand in hand with economic – that works for all of the people of the region.

The national need for innovation-led regional growth

Innovation is the key route by which research translates into societal benefit. It is through accelerating the time between discovery and real-world deployment that universities in the twenty-first century can genuinely make an impact and fulfil their civic role. Unit M is designed to make that transition even swifter.

Unit M and the UoM's embracing of the innovation agenda is a response to the myriad of interlinked yet urgent economic and social challenges the UK faces. High public debt, squeezed public services and regional inequalities (see Chapter 3) necessitate faster and more inclusive growth across all parts of the country. The largest cities – those with outsized impact in their regions – are critical to rebalancing growth by driving improvements in public services and living standards, and the fundamental driver of economic growth is innovation. Turning ideas into real-world impact via the introduction of new products, processes and improvements is the fastest and most meaningful way of shifting the UK's economy. A step change in regional innovation will dramatically accelerate prosperity and provide a more inclusive model of growth.

At a local and national level the spotlight on universities as catalysts of regional growth via innovation is timely. The Government has committed to new statutory Local Growth Plans that will be developed by local leaders, working with universities and major employers, to identify growth sectors. The Government has also created Skills England, with a mandate to deliver the skills needed for its Industrial Strategy, including by better integrating further and higher education. Mayor of Greater Manchester (GM) Andy Burnham's 2024 manifesto also commits to 'making Greater Manchester the leading innovation ecosystem outside of the Golden Triangle'.[5]

New technologies

The renewed focus on innovation also comes at a time when new technologies are driving an unparalleled scale and pace of transformation, challenge and opportunity. This creates an urgency to the innovation agenda locally and globally. While UoM and the wider region are well represented in these new-frontier technologies, both will need to innovate rapidly to keep up with the pace of change. As the proliferation of these frontier technologies accelerates, with increased demand comes significantly reduced cost. This will remove barriers to adoption and participation and bring unrivalled opportunities to address major societal challenges such as tackling climate change, revolutionising healthcare or democratising education.

In Manchester, additional urgency on this agenda locally is created by the scale and severity of societal challenges that the University's neighbouring communities and wider region face, which could in part be overcome through adoption and application of these frontier technologies. However, these new technologies also bring new types and levels of risk as they become available to bad actors who have easy access to technologies that have the potential to create individual and societal harm. Part of the innovation challenge for universities will precisely be in terms of how best to counter these technological threats.

Innovation increasingly matters in terms of student experience too, because exposure to innovation provides an enriched learning experience. Studies continually show that today's students are more than ever seeking entrepreneurial pathways both during their studies and after graduation. Young people want to be engaged in shaping the future of the cities, regions and towns they live in. They are actively looking to change the world and improve their own lives and the lives of those around them. For instance, a survey by Forbes found that up to 84 per cent of Gen Z are planning to start their own business or side hustle, and the number of businesses started by young founders increased by 400 per cent from 2021 to 2022.[6]

Young people are looking for brands, employers and institutions which can support them in their careers or business ventures, that embody their values and which enable their voices to be heard. The term 'innovation economy' doesn't mean anything to this important audience. Instead, they want to see innovation and collaborations with universities, local businesses and organisations that make a real difference to their own lives and the communities they live in. By making UoM more porous and increasing connectivity between the institution and its surrounding areas, Unit M will help make this a reality.

Manchester's untapped innovation potential

City and regional ecosystems facilitate strong connections between the main actors involved in the innovation process, including universities, research and technology organisations, venture capitalists and investors, and businesses. Such ecosystems generate mutually beneficial flows of knowledge, finance, people and services between them. The opportunity to catalyse Manchester's innovation ecosystem is huge and, so far, relatively untapped.

Manchester has been transformed since the mid-1990s and is one of the country's fastest-growing cities. It has many of the attributes of a high-performing innovation ecosystem, but it cannot yet claim to be world class. Its huge potential to drive innovation, and therefore growth, across the region and the UK is not yet fully realised. International comparator cities with similar economic histories and structures to Manchester, such as Pittsburgh and Munich, are two striking examples of cities which have successfully created strong innovation ecosystems.

Productivity is stubbornly low and remains a challenge in Manchester. The Productivity Institute, based at Alliance Manchester Business School (AMBS), identifies three key problems that need to be tackled: low investment by the public and private sectors; lack of knowledge diffusion; and institutional fragmentation. Industry R&D spend similarly lags other regions. Businesses in the Manchester city region spend less on R&D than the UK average and significantly less than firms in the highest-performing innovation ecosystems. Business R&D investment is 1 per cent of GDP in Greater Manchester and Cheshire (UK: 1.2 per cent; OECD: 2.7 per cent), due to the region having a predominantly SME-based economy, few R&D functions of major national and international firms and a lack of large 'prime' manufacturers.[7]

Unlocking R&D

Developing new, more flexible and responsive approaches to work with SMEs to unlock R&D spending will be important, as will engaging with large R&D-intensive companies outside of the Greater Manchester area (e.g. the cluster of specialist chemicals and life sciences companies in Cheshire and Liverpool, and the aerospace cluster in Lancashire) and attracting new global R&D frontier companies to the region. More business-facing resources need to be put in place and there needs to be more focus on helping firms to adopt existing (not just create new) innovations. Deep-tech start-ups are the driving force of future R&D investment, but Manchester is not generating as many as would be expected and the number trails comparable cities. Being more responsive and agile to industry requirements across the entire company life cycle will be critical to unlock more R&D and innovation investment.

Skills is the other challenge holding back growth, and the one most often cited by employers in the region. Access to student talent is often the first reason for firms to engage with universities, and is an important foundation for building future, deeper relationships. Student start-ups spawn an entrepreneurial mindset that can also help students become intrapreneurs – i.e. champions of innovation within a university. UoM's undergraduate and postgraduate programmes, executive education and new flexible learning programmes give it a strong platform on which to build, but it will have to keep innovating to keep pace with a rapidly changing policy and business environment.

The innovation opportunity

As I have touched on, Greater Manchester has many of the assets that make it an attractive location for UK and international businesses looking to relocate or scale-up, and it is regularly ranked as one of the UK's most liveable cities, with good access to world-class talent and good availability of affordable space for manufacturing, office and lab uses. Being able to partner with the UoM is a key aspect of the 'sales pitch' for the region's inward investment agencies and property agents. Taking a more proactive approach to attracting R&D-intensive inward investment to the region – for instance by engaging early with companies looking to relocate to the city region to put in place the R&D and skills programmes they need to thrive – would benefit the country, the region, the city and the University.

The city region's innovation map is also changing. Significant development is planned on the Oxford Road Corridor over the next fifteen years to 2040 alongside innovation-focused schemes in other parts of the city centre such as the creative and digital incubator at Enterprise City and the Government's digital hub (and future home of Government Communications Headquarters) at Central Retail Park. Outside the city centre, major developments at Atom Valley in North East Manchester, the Ashton Moss Mayoral Development Zone and MIX Manchester at Manchester Airport are focused on manufacturing and life sciences innovation. Ensuring UoM appropriately derives the full potential for impact from these schemes will require ways of working with place-makers and local authorities.

Greater Manchester also has a strong record of public–private collaboration, which provides a strong platform for universities to deliver enhanced impact at pace and scale. The Civic Universities Agreement launched in 2022 brings together the region's five universities with the ten local authorities and Mayor's Office, and has made progress in aligning organisational strategies and programmes.[8] Innovation GM also brings together business, universities and public sector agencies across the city region and has made progress in developing an innovation strategy for the region and attracting additional public innovation investment into Greater Manchester, such as the Innovation Accelerator and Investment Zone programmes.

The University of Manchester's pivotal role

As I have said, UoM is the region's single most significant innovation asset. Its potential to address the challenges the region faces and contribute positively to drive growth and prosperity over coming years is nationally significant. No other organisation has the scale, civic mission, long-term time horizons, credibility and capability to do so. Without the full support of UoM, it will be difficult for the region to achieve its true social and economic potential. UoM was England's first civic university and has deep roots in serving and catalysing the region's industry and economy. Today, its annual £270 million research income is the sixth highest in the UK and, as already mentioned, accounts for 93 per cent of all research income in Greater Manchester. Incredibly, this would actually put the university in the UK's top twenty R&D spenders if it were a private sector company.

There is a local and national imperative for UoM to utilise its extensive innovation resources to supercharge the next era of regional growth. Regional innovation is also a central component of its social responsibility agenda, helping to deliver its vision to create prosperous communities by increasing economic wellbeing, developing new sectors, innovating, and improving productivity for all people and all areas of the city region. The University has fundamental strengths that make it well suited to driving Manchester's innovation ecosystem. For instance, it has one of the broadest ranges of research disciplines of any UK university, and this aligns with Greater Manchester's diverse economic structure, containing as it does a sophisticated mix of industries and supply chains. Within this complex economy, the region has identified industrial specialisms in areas such as health innovation (including life sciences), advanced materials, digital, creative industries, energy (especially nuclear) and business, management and accounting – all sectors where UoM has major strengths and concentrations of research excellence. Indeed, UoM has received significant investment from local and national Government and invested its own funds (matched with industry) to create regionally focused innovation centres with the potential to drive these key frontier sectors. These include the Turing Innovation Catalyst, the Graphene Engineering Innovation Centre, the Sustainable Materials Innovation Hub and the Christabel Pankhurst Institute for Health Technology.

Collaboration

Interdisciplinary collaboration also supports innovation. UoM's unique selling point is not tied to a single technology or sector. Instead, it lies in its ability to drive interdisciplinary collaboration and join up R&D, training, social responsibility and innovation activities across the institution, and through its strong regional partnerships. Increasingly, businesses (particularly scaling businesses) do not want access to one technology specialism, they also want access to a broader set of capabilities which can be delivered only by an interdisciplinary approach. In this regard UoM's corporate structure – which facilitates interdisciplinary approaches to research, teaching and innovation – puts it in a great position to capitalise on these opportunities and support all components of a company's scale-up journey.

As mentioned, UoM naturally has an essential role to play in meeting the region's skills needs too. However, linking students more deeply with the innovation economy will be critical, and UoM needs to develop new forms of provision. Creating partnerships with other leading innovation ecosystems in the UK and globally can be transformational for UoM, the region and the UK, and UoM has the capabilities that are vital to successfully lead these partnerships for the region. A strong and deep relationship with the city of Manchester and Greater Manchester will therefore be essential for UoM to capitalise on the economic opportunities on its doorstep.

Unit M: supercharging the University's impact

The next few years will therefore be crucial to delivering the UK's innovation ambition. For UoM this means ensuring that it remains relevant and competitive at the innovation frontier, creating new productive partnerships with the global companies which will come to dominate these sectors, as well as navigating the complex ethical challenges that developing these new technologies will bring. It will also need to play its part in creating the foundations for a more productive economy by supporting productivity improvements in firms and sectors not at the technology frontier. It is in this context that UoM launched Unit M to significantly grow the size, calibre and impact of its innovation ecosystem.

The genesis of Unit M lies in the 2024 Regional Innovation Review, commissioned by UoM in the wake of the unprecedented transformation of business and society, and urgent crises in climate, health and education. The review aimed to better understand the regional innovation picture and what role the University could play in terms of driving forward the city and region's economy. The central recommendation was that UoM establish a clear strategic framework for its regional innovation ambition to provide it with a solid foundation on which to drive decisions, and to coordinate activity both across the University and with regional partners. As UoM's specialist innovation capability, Unit M provides a layer of agility and commerciality around the innovation agenda, while allowing the core of UoM to continue to focus its innovation efforts on research and teaching excellence. It places the regional innovation agenda at the heart of UoM's next chapter, while it also diversifies commercial revenue streams and risk profile. It will elevate UoM and its home city to its rightful place on the global innovation map.

Addressing key challenges

Unit M will address key national challenges in productivity, sustainability and economic inclusion by working with partners to tackle all parts of the innovation process, from R&D to innovation adoption, to talent and skills. It will also coordinate the regional innovation agenda across UoM, catalysing the innovation-led start-up and scale-up community, developing incubator and pilot-scale facilities on campus and with partners and delivering accelerator programmes that use University capabilities. Student start-ups, including from UoM's pool of more than 5,000 PhD students, are a relatively untapped source of innovation-led start-ups. 'Spin ins', early-stage companies which choose to partner with the University to grow their business despite not having a prior institutional connection, also offer opportunities.

Alongside this activity, Unit M will help develop regional innovation clusters which connect University research, innovation and training capabilities, and students, to innovation-focused developments. These will focus on key sectors, such as AI, materials, biotech and healthtech in sites including Atom Valley and the Sister innovation district in Manchester. Unit M is also designed to bridge the gap with other participants in the innovation economy, enabling the University to be much more flexible to industry R&D demand. It is building new strategic innovation partnerships to attract new businesses to the region and grow existing innovation-intensive companies.

Additionally, it will help deliver place-based innovation ecosystem prototyping projects, providing agile capacity to help drive forward large-scale and/or highly innovative new University-led initiatives. This includes the UK's first cross-UK innovation partnership, between Manchester and Cambridge. There is a national imperative to learn how to develop cross-cluster partnerships that bring together capabilities and allow the UK to compete globally. This progressive new model of place-to-place collaboration has the aim of creating a hyper-connected, high-performing set of innovation ecosystems that amplify what each can achieve independently to drive economic growth for the UK. Led by the universities of Cambridge and Manchester – and housed in Unit M – it aims to strengthen innovation networks, accelerate scale-up growth, drive private sector investment into R&D and attract new foreign direct investment to the UK. Unit M is also supporting the delivery of ecosystem prototype projects that have the potential to be applied much more widely in the future to maximise impact through initiatives like the Centre of Excellence on In-Silico Regulatory Science and Innovation.[9] The Centre is exploring how to make medical product testing and approval processes faster, safer and more cost-effective, an innovation that could one day have global impact.

As UoM's voice on innovation Unit M also has a convening role, leading strategic engagement with other regional stakeholders such as the Mayor's Office, Greater Manchester Combined Authority and local councils. Alongside these partners and others, it will tell Manchester's innovation story – past, present and, most importantly, future – on a global stage.

What this means for Alliance Manchester Business School

At the heart of AMBS's mission is training the current and next generation of business leaders. Poor-quality management and leadership skills is one of the key challenges for the UK's economic underperformance, and the School has a central role to play in driving future prosperity. Without great leaders, even the best innovations will not thrive. The School is home to the Masood Entrepreneurship Centre, UoM's centre for student entrepreneurship and start-ups, which provides teaching and skills development for students, recent graduates and staff, while it also runs a Scale-up Forum, a peer-to-peer network for business leaders to explore common challenges, share experiences and connect with UoM and its partners. The School also houses UoM's Executive Education Centre, which delivers professional development programmes including short courses, senior leader apprenticeships and customised programmes. As mentioned, it is also home to The Productivity Institute, a UK-wide research organisation exploring what productivity means for business, workers and communities, and also to the Manchester Institute of Innovation Research, which focuses on the study of science, technology and innovation policy and management, including regional innovation.

Unit M will therefore be working in close collaboration with AMBS to deliver the University's innovation ambition, outlined in our 2035 strategy. The breadth of interdisciplinary research and talent that exists in AMBS, as well as deep collaboration with industry, will make a significant contribution to the region's future prosperity.

Summary

I believe that UoM's new approach to regional innovation can, within ten years, put it among the top ten globally for innovation, while elevating Manchester into the top twenty global innovation cities.

For the University this will result in more high-impact innovation partnerships with industry, leading to international recognition for our ecosystem's strength. It will also benefit from increased levels of interdisciplinary research aimed at addressing business and societal innovation challenges and an enhanced student experience. For the businesses we partner with, it will result in greater support for their innovation ambitions through simplified access to the University's scale, research expertise and global network. Companies will gain from a more responsive relationship than they typically have with academic institutions, and innovation-led clusters will help start-ups to scale and existing SMEs to grow, and provide the right environment for new companies to come to the region.

For the region it will result in an innovation-led economy that creates good jobs, higher pay and improved productivity. It will also narrow the gap between Manchester and the UK's leading city regions, improving the life chances of local residents. And, crucially, it will also empower the region to fulfil its critical role in the country's growth mission.

Key recommendations

- The time is now for universities to step up as catalysts of place-based growth and leverage place-based assets, and this is a moment for UoM and AMBS to act with urgency on the regional innovation agenda and be ambitious. Actions during the next critical five-year window (2025–30) will have implications for the University and region for decades to come.
- A focus on cracking the innovation adoption challenge is critical to addressing UK productivity. The proposals set out in the Regional Innovation Review can, over the coming ten-year window (2025–35), elevate the University to be one of the best in the world while at the same time transporting Manchester to be a globally leading city.
- Skills needs continue to hold back economic growth in the region. Undergraduate and postgraduate programmes, executive education

and new flexible learning programmes at UoM and AMBS provide a strong platform on which to build, but the institutions will have to keep innovating to keep pace with a rapidly changing policy and business environment.

Notes

1. Russell Group (2024) 'University research and innovation generates £38bn for the UK economy', *Russell Group*, 28 February, www.russellgroup.ac.uk/news/university-research-and-innovation-generates-ps38bn-uk-economy (accessed 19 March 2025).
2. University of Manchester (2021) *Research Excellence Framework 2021*, www.manchester.ac.uk/research/impact/ref-2021/ (accessed 13 March 2025).
3. University of Manchester (n.d.) *Unrivalled Social and Environmental Impact*, www.manchester.ac.uk/about/social-responsibility/sdgs/ (accessed 13 March 2025).
4. University of Manchester (2024) 'University of Manchester launches Unit M to supercharge inclusive growth', 8 October, www.manchester.ac.uk/about/news/university-of-manchester-launches-unit-m-to-supercharge-inclusive-growth/ (accessed 6 May 2025).
5. A. Burnham (2024) *Andy Burnham Manifesto 2024: Greater Manchester Leading the Way*, https://andyformayor.co.uk/manifesto/ (accessed 13 March 2025).
6. M. Perna (2024) 'Why Gen Z is thriving in the entrepreneurial life', *Forbes*, 18 June, www.forbes.com/sites/markcperna/2024/06/18/gen-z-thriving-entrepreneurship/ (accessed 6 May 2025).
7. OECD (2024) *OECD Economic Surveys: UK 2024*, www.oecd.org/content/dam/oecd/en/publications/reports/2024/09/oecd-economic-surveys-united-kingdom-2024_82b39666/709e70b8-en.pdf (accessed 19 March 2025).
8. University of Manchester (2022) *Civic University Agreement*, 25 October, www.manchester.ac.uk/about/social-responsibility/civic/civic-agreement/ (accessed 13 March 2025).
9. University of Manchester (2025) 'UK's first In-silico Regulatory Science and Innovation Centre of Excellence gets green light', 31 January, www.manchester.ac.uk/about/news/uks-first-in-silico-regulatory-science-and-innovation-centre-of-excellence-gets-green-light/ (accessed 6 May 2025).

3
CITIES, REGIONS AND TURNING AROUND THE NORTH

Terry Leahy and Philip McCann

Introduction

This chapter examines the case for a pan-regional approach to building global city regions in the northern regions of England. In order to do this, we first discuss the current nature of the UK city and regional economic landscape and then move on to explain how this landscape has arisen since the mid-1980s. We follow this with discussion of how the financial and capital markets perceive UK cities and regions, and then go on to outline the key features of the current UK governance reform and devolution agenda. Finally we discuss the key elements involved in building a global region across northern cities, with a major emphasis on the need for coordinating mechanisms and institutions, what these might look like and how they might operate. We end with some brief conclusions and recommendations.

The UK city and regional economic landscape

Regional productivity inequalities in the UK are today among the highest in the industrialised world. As is widely documented, across multiple dimensions London and its hinterland display some of the highest productivity and prosperity indices anywhere in the industrialised world. At the same time, almost half of the UK population today live in areas which are no more productive than many parts of Eastern Europe such as the Czech Republic or Slovakia, are poorer than the poorest US states of Mississippi and West Virginia and have a multi-dimensional quality of life which is akin to US states such as Alabama or Tennessee.[1]

Since the mid-1980s, the UK has been internally decoupling on almost every socio-economic dimension as well as productivity, including social mobility, job opportunities and the quality of work, and, most markedly, healthy life expectancy.[2] Moreover, these enormous differences occur in a country which is smaller than the US states of Wyoming and Michigan, with England being no bigger than the US states of Louisiana and Alabama. The scale of these national productivity and prosperity inequalities over such short geographical distances is unprecedented among the industrialised world and points to specific experience of the UK as being rather different to many other countries.[3]

Distortions

The economic geography of urban growth and development in the UK has faced many significant distortions in recent decades. Up until the late 1970s, the city size distribution for UK urban areas followed the standard Zipf's Law distributions evident in many countries. The insight of Zipf's Law was that investment opportunities are evenly spread across the regions of a country, such that growth rates over a long time period were independent of the prevailing city size, resulting in a very regular ordering of city sizes. In other words, for most of the nineteenth and twentieth centuries, the relative population sizes of UK cities followed patterns which were typical in other industrialised countries. But from the early 1980s onward the UK city size distributions started to diverge from what are typically observed in other countries.

This shift was most notable when measured against the effective economic size of the cities, rather than simply their population sizes. Since the mid-1980s, London has come to dominate the UK economic system to an extent which is unprecedented by any large city in any other large Organisation for Economic Co-operation and Development (OECD) country.[4] For much of the post-war period up until the late-1980s, the London economy exhibited productivity levels of approximately 23–28 per cent above the UK regional average, with many other regions exhibiting similar productivity levels to each other, between 90 per cent and 105 per cent of the UK average.

However, by the years immediately preceding the 2008 global financial crisis, the London productivity premium over the UK as a whole had already risen to something of the order of 75 per cent over the UK regional averages. Meanwhile, other UK industrial and highly urbanised regions displayed productivity levels falling to something of the order of 75–90 per cent of the UK average. In other words, within two decades spanning the turn of the twenty-first century, London's productivity levels had risen to some twice those of many other UK cities, and the UK regional economic system had become highly unbalanced.

Interregional mobility

Across the OECD, many countries have faced regional deindustrialisation allied with interregional mobility away from less prosperous regions and towards more prosperous regions. More highly educated and younger people with high levels of human capital are typically the most mobile cohorts of the population and, as in other OECD countries, these migration patterns are also evident in the UK, although their scale is often misunderstood and somewhat exaggerated. However, in the UK, interregional migration flows have barely changed since the 1970s, while the UK regional productivity shocks have far outweighed the interregional movements of human capital.[5] Today, the dispersion in UK regional productivity variations far outweighs the regional dispersions in workforce education and skills at either the upper or lower extremes.[6] This suggests that UK interregional productivity differences are a result of far more complex forces than human capital migration alone.

The growth of UK regional divides over four decades

A wide array of evidence suggests that the four-decade-long internal economic decoupling of the UK reflects a specific combination of geography, globalisation and governance.[7] In terms of geography, the UK is the only large OECD country in which the vast majority of all trade-related flows of goods, services, knowledge, finance and transportation pass through the capital city region.

This extreme economic geography monocentricity creates an automatic inflationary bottleneck which acts as a break on economic growth in other regions, as former Governor of the Bank of England Eddie George implicitly acknowledged almost three decades ago.[8]

At the same time, the economic shocks associated with the advent of modern globalisation in the 1980s were highly asymmetric, in that adverse shocks were prevalent in the regions of the Midlands and the North, whereas positive economic shocks were primarily evident in the South and South-East of England. While these asymmetric shocks were taking place, from 1985 the UK governance and institutional system was also undergoing a major centralisation shift, in which national economic and public policy became highly top-down, space-blind and 'one-size-fits-all' in design and orchestration. This centralisation rendered the UK governance system as being largely incapable of responding to various shocks to different regions, and many regions suffered as a result of a lack of any meaningful place-based policy logic attuned to their specific challenges.[9]

In hindsight it is possible to make some sense of the prevailing thinking which dominated governments in the 1980s. For most of the nineteenth and twentieth centuries, industrialised economies experienced national economic growth fundamentally as a regional convergence process.[10] In other words, as national economies grew, the less productive and prosperous regions of the economy were automatically catching up the more productive and prosperous regions of that same national economy as deregulated markets offered new investment opportunities at competitive prices.

The role of London

This phenomenon was more or less ubiquitous and, indeed, by the late 1970s the UK as a whole displayed one of the least unbalanced and most equal interregional economic systems in the industrialised world.[11] As such, UK policy thinking in the 1980s and 1990s was largely driven by an assumption that London must be well served with new infrastructure befitting of its role as a capital city and a gateway to global markets. Alongside this all other regulatory structures must be well designed and well enforced in order to spread the benefits of economic development everywhere. The assumption was that these conditions were sufficient to ensure that UK-wide competition processes would themselves naturally drive knowledge diffusion and dissemination into all parts of the economy, which in turn would drive national growth and regional convergence processes. Unfortunately, this was not what happened.

As already mentioned, the first evidence of UK interregional divergence, and in particular the start of the London economy pulling away from the rest of the UK in terms of regional productivity, appears in the official data in around 1988.[12] By the early 1990s, the pulling away of London from the rest of the UK regional economic system was very pronounced. This rapidly growing relative dominance of London over the UK urban system also took place at precisely the same time that the UK economy as a whole started to experience underlying shifts in regional productivity patterns away from convergence to divergence.

As well as the lion's share of private investment, over four decades London and its close hinterland received the overwhelming majority of productivity-enhancing public investments, which in turn galvanised additional local private investments.[13] In contrast, rather than catalysing further surges of private investments across the rest of the UK, London and its hinterland largely decoupled from the rest of the UK on many socio-economic dimensions, and government centralisation was a major part of the reason why.[14]

However, at the time there was no comparative data on different countries, so the newly emerging economic geography of the UK economy could not be meaningfully compared with, or assessed in the light of the experience of, other countries. At the time, our understanding of these local and regional productivity imbalances thus remained very limited.

Indeed, in hindsight, major government reports from the early 2000s display a remarkable lack of awareness, both of the scale of the issues which had already been playing out for many years within the UK and of the extent to which these issues were themselves related to governance.[15] Today, in many ways, the UK has become a 'hub, no spokes' economy, in which many of the major knowledge generation and knowledge spillover processes operate only locally within London and its close regional hinterland, with the rest of the UK largely blocked out of many of these productivity-enhancing mechanisms.[16]

Capital market and investor perceptions of UK cities and regions

This extreme economic monocentricity inadvertently but increasingly creates an 'insider–outsider' pattern to the UK economy, in which many types of investors are likely to view investing in the UK as being a choice between investing in London and its immediate hinterland region versus the rest of the UK or other countries.

Today, the vast majority of corporate headquarter functions are located in the capital city.[17] Although Scotland and Wales still retain some headquarter functions, as does the wider South region, the lack of corporate headquarter functions is particularly marked in the Midlands and Northern England.[18] By 2015, none of the FTSE 100 English businesses based north of Birmingham when the index began in 1984 were still in the FTSE.[19] Similarly, London accounts for 50 per cent of all venture capital (VC) and, combined with the South-East of England, the share rises to two-thirds of all VC, while the remaining one-third is spread across the rest of the UK.[20] This financial centralisation has increased markedly in recent decades, such that outside of Scotland the UK has no local or devolved banking system, and many parts of the UK have few or no angel finance or VC systems.[21] The centralisation of the UK state on so many dimensions was also clearly reflected in the UK's response to the 2008 global financial crisis.

2008 crisis

Prior to the 2008 crisis, the spreads in risk-pricing across UK cities and regions were tiny. However, the dramatic events of the crisis led to a sudden change from an environment of risk to one of radical uncertainty in which investors were unable to apportion and price in risk in the economy.[22] This led to a global 'flight to safety' of investment capital into gold, Japanese government bonds (even though Japan had not grown for two decades) and other ostensibly safe assets. In the UK, the extreme post-crisis centralisation of the UK economy was almost exactly reflected in how capital markets priced in risk in UK cities and regions in the wake of the crisis, with investors' priorities shifting suddenly from seeking growth to preserving value.

This was manifested in a surge of capital into London and its hinterland and dramatically reduced prices. Real estate asset owners located in London found that their collateral leveraging positions improved sharply, and they were able to access the increased capital at very favourable prices. In contrast, most other cities and regions of the UK immediately shifted from being perceived as 'blue chip' investment landscapes to 'junk bond' arenas, with shrinking available capital, declining real estate collateral positions and residual capital being priced exorbitantly. Most of the UK is still stuck in this 'junk bond' tier, over fifteen years after the crisis, and places which faced these adverse capital shocks subsequently faced falling productivity and population growth.[23]

Long-lasting shocks

These city and regional capital market shock effects are long lasting. Today, the UK regional spreads in risk pricing and in investment yields are of the order of 250 basis points, with the spreads between city centres being of the order of 300 basis points.[24] These spreads are akin to the current market risk spreads between UK gilts and the sovereigns offered by Romania or Chile.[25] Moreover, these capital market shocks to UK cities and regions undermined the efficacy of much of national economic policymaking. London responded directly and effectively to the emergency introduction of quantitative easing (QE) and rapidly regained its 'blue chip' risk pricing, whereas most of the country was entirely unaffected by QE.[26] Indeed, a careful examination of the City and regional responses to QE shows that most of the UK is nowadays entirely unaffected in any beneficial way by monetary policy.[27]

The governance reform and devolution agenda

This leads to a profound problem for UK economic governance. If monetary policy is entirely ineffective outside of London, and the space for additional fiscal resources is largely non-existent, then the only policy-related avenue for generating growth in the wider UK economy is that of governance reform.

The city-region governance reform agenda originates in the later years of the Gordon Brown Labour Government and the early years of the Coalition Government from 2010. The Conservative Government of David Cameron accelerated the process under the leadership of Chancellor George Osborne and the guidance of Michael Heseltine and Jim O'Neill. This was further bolstered by the Levelling Up agenda, spurred by the 2022 White Paper *Levelling Up the United Kingdom* under the leadership of Michael Gove and Andy Haldane.

This was a response in part to the 'geography of discontent' evident in the 2016 Brexit vote, in which regional inequalities and politics became intrinsically fused in a manner which had hitherto been somewhat more opaque.[28] Importantly, in the years since the Brexit vote the public conversations about regional inequalities changed fundamentally, with a growing and widespread acceptance in public and media arenas that UK regional inequalities were exceptional by the standards of advanced economies, and that addressing these challenges needed to be not only a national priority but also undertaken in a manner which would be markedly different from previous policy approaches.

Change of mindset

On this point one of the most important policy shifts required a change of mindset on the part of Whitehall, something which has still only partially been achieved, and this concerns the Whitehall view of governance control. A longstanding and deeply embedded grain of thought in policymakers, especially in HM Treasury but also in other Whitehall departments, is the notion that decentralised governance inhibits growth, whereas a more centrally orchestrated and tightly controlled top-down governance system is advantageous for national economic growth.

Similar lines of thinking also assumed or even asserted that significant differences in regional growth were necessary or even desirable to drive national growth. The exact origins of these lines of thinking are unclear, but they became widespread during the decades that the UK government system itself became more centralised. In reality, cross-country evidence shows that there is no relationship whatsoever between governance centralisation or decentralisation and national economic growth, or regional inequality and growth.[29] Rather, the internal economic geography of growth differs markedly between different types of governance systems, with national economic growth being shared more evenly across regions in a devolved governance system.

However, even by the standards of unitary governance system countries, the regional inequalities in the UK are extreme.[30] The fifteen-year post-crisis combination of sluggish national annual productivity growth allied with extreme interregional productivity inequalities implies that the increasingly centralised governance trajectory of the UK since the 1980s was a mistake on many levels.

Narrowing risk premia

An important indication that devolved governance has the potential to foster stronger local economic growth comes from very recent evidence, in which the two largest devolved city-regions, namely the West Midlands and Greater Manchester areas, have displayed rapidly narrowing risk premia and investment yields towards London levels. Since 2020, market investors appear to be increasing their confidence and trust in the overall investment climate in these two places, and there are many arguments which suggest that this is indeed the whole point of strong and well-designed local devolved governance institutions.

Devolved institutions potentially can provide locally specific contact points and access to key decision makers for investors, ensuring that strategic discussions are situated at appropriate levels which are large enough to be meaningful, while also small enough to be relevant to the local context. Building confidence on the part of the investment community in those cities and regions which have faced adverse and repeated economic shocks is crucial for turning around cities.[31]

Building a global region across northern cities

Regalvanising and regenerating northern cities is a long and slow process which needs to be carefully constructed. Northern cities tend to be located very close to each other, so this offers the opportunity for building pan-northern economies based on the better coordination and linking of cities as a counterweight to the London agglomeration. Indeed, as Andy Haldane has argued, today global regions comprised of groups of cities are playing an increasingly important part in national growth and development, marshalling scale-related productivity effects and providing investors with multiple investment opportunities allied with the infrastructure to make those investments viable and profitable in the long run.[32]

The city-regions of the North and Midlands account for almost a third of the UK population, but the longstanding underperformance must be addressed as a key part of the national growth strategy. The challenge to build global regions in the North and Midlands of the UK involves rebuilding economies of scale at the individual city level, and especially in the central business districts of the cities, and also linking up these areas in a manner in which the sum is greater than the parts.

In order for this to be the case, the aim to build global regions in the North and Midlands therefore requires new means of coordination aimed at building scale within and between UK cities. Many of the major economic challenges faced by northern regions are not constrained within individual cities. These challenges include attracting foreign direct investment, deploying environmental technologies, upgrading advanced manufacturing, building local and regional innovation systems, ensuring skills pipelines in new technologies, reorganising transportation and logistics systems and increasing the supply of investment capital to SMEs across a broader range of cities.

However, there are also various UK-specific challenges to building global regions in the North which must be overcome, of which three are the most important.

First, the UK is alone among OECD countries in that there are no systematic scale-related productivity advantages, in the sense that once London is removed, greater urban scale is not associated with higher levels of productivity, as is the case in almost all other industrialised countries.[33] A manifestation of this is that, unlike large US cities which display increasing returns to higher education, constant or increasing returns to graduate education are only really evident in the London economy, with other UK regions typically displaying diminishing returns to higher-education human capital.[34] This is a curious and highly problematic feature of the UK economy, and in all likelihood relates to how interaction between the land-use planning system, the green belt framework and the increasing governance and infrastructure centralisation around London has played out since the 1970s.[35] At the same time, UK city commercial centres outside of London are typically much smaller than might be expected, given the overall population sizes of the cities, especially in terms of knowledge-intensive activities.[36] The scale of people having high levels of commuting accessibility to the city centres is also much smaller than their overall urban population levels imply.[37]

Second, the economic underperformance of the large urban areas outside of the South-East of England means that today's productivity and prosperity gaps between large urban areas, smaller urban areas, towns, suburbs and rural areas are among the very lowest in the industrialised world. In a typical urban and regional economic system, large cities would be more productive than smaller cities, which in turn would be more productive than towns, which in turn would be more productive than rural regions. However, while these relationships hold in the South-East of England, outside of the South-East there is almost no difference in terms of the productivity performance of different types of places.[38] Nor are there any productivity growth-related advantages to being an urban area, outside of the London economy.[39] Indeed, in many UK regions large urban areas are actually less productive than smaller urban areas or even rural areas, and this has remained the case for more than twenty years.[40] The widespread lack of urban advantages is also reflected by the fact that there is a smaller difference in population growth patterns between urban and rural areas in the UK than in almost any other OECD country.[41] This is a phenomenon which is almost unique to the UK, and again accounts for the fact that, once London is removed, there is no systematic relationship between urban scale and productivity or prosperity.

Third, much of the UK exhibits no meaningful meso-levels of governance, and even those that are emerging – such as the mayoral combined authorities – still have relatively very limited powers and are very small by international standards. Meso-levels of governance operate at a tier in between central and local governments and are a key feature of the institutional landscape of most industrialised countries. Meso-levels of economic governance in other OECD countries are determined variously by states, *länder*, provinces, cantons and metropolitan authorities, many of which have significant legal and financial powers, including automatically assigned taxes from the central state, locally devolved taxes, significant legal authority and decision-making autonomy from central government. Meso-level economic governance institutions across the OECD typically range from three million to seven million people, such that our two largest city-regions, Greater Manchester and the West Midlands, are only just at the lower bounds of this range. Even today, the scale at which most of England's devolved economic functions are being framed is equivalent to what is typically observed in small countries with populations which are a fraction of the size of the UK.[42]

Cities that have turned around

Overcoming these challenges requires vision, leadership and trust building on the part of key actors, and convincing progress can come about only on the basis of significant changes to an array of different interlocking elements, including enhancing the offer for global investors, the stimulation of local capital markets, skills retraining, much greater discretionary powers over local infrastructure provision, land-use and planning matters, the upgrading of heritage, the rediscovery of industrial philanthropy and a concerted effort toward city marketing, branding and information provision. Examples of these types of large-scale and comprehensive approaches to 'turning around' cities include Pittsburgh, Windsor Ontario, Dortmund, Duisburg, Bilbao, Lille and Newcastle, New South Wales.[43] In each case, coordinated multi-level governance actions between the cities and their respective states, provinces or autonomous regions underpinned comprehensive and long-term economic redevelopment strategies spanning all relevant arenas and aimed at enhancing investor confidence. These cities are again globally competitive.

In contrast, the city-region combined authority model in the UK is still very small by OECD-wide standards in terms of investment promotion, and other solutions need to be sought.[44] Most of the individual mayoral combined authorities are too small to carry this role alone, lacking any multi-level regional backing, or any meaningful discretionary powers over their long-term fiscal base. One obvious option, therefore, is for the construction of pan-regional coordinating bodies which can better link and scale-up the investment offerings of northern cities. Such bodies need not necessarily be designed or mandated from above, but can be established and nurtured by the city-regions themselves working together, in a manner akin to the joint workings of local governments in the formation of combined authorities.

The pooling of resources and powers at the local scale has been a catalyst for the establishment of the mayoral combined authorities, and similar principles could underpin the establishment of pan-regional institutions aimed at fostering inward investment. These principles need to be scaled up institutionally and geographically in order to better reflect and capture much larger market potential for investors.

Legislative framework

The introduction of a legislative framework to incentivise these types of arrangements could be a major catalyst for the shift towards a more global region model for the cities of the North and Midlands. As is the case with other large urban concentrations across the industrialised world, northern cities therefore need powers which would allow them to coordinate activities across a wide range of economic arenas, including attracting foreign direct investment, supply chain development, fostering environmental transitions and coordinating research activities.

The current devolution arrangements contain few provisions for this type of engagement. Yet, in order to underpin these activities across a broader scale, northern cities need to build the institutional architecture to facilitate and maximise credit provision into local businesses, and especially R&D-intensive start-ups and SMEs, and also to develop coordinated cross-jurisdictional infrastructure provision and land supply strategies. These two issues are interrelated. On the one hand, good-quality land supply acts as a facilitator of investment, by providing appropriate facilities for locating business investments. Also, if well managed, good-quality land supply can act as a collateral channel for additional investments. Other parts of the industrialised world deploy a suite of strategies and institutions to simultaneously facilitate these processes, including the establishment and operation of urban wealth funds, the local activities of development banks, the ability to raise capital directly on the international markets without recourse to central government, the deployment of pan-regional strategic land-use planning frameworks and the coordination of regional export promotion and investment attraction by 'one-stop-shop' trade-promotion agencies.

In other OECD countries, the activities of these types of bodies and institutions are also closely supported by chambers of commerce which take on significant legal responsibilities in order to foster the local business and skills-related ecosystems. The creation of such coordinating bodies or platforms in the UK would also require that the economic development strategies of the different city-regions be closely aligned in key respects. For example, the distribution of land suitable for different types of commercial investments will differ markedly between city-regions, as will land suitable for housing and the accessibility to different types of transport and communications infrastructure. Labour markets and research institutions will also differ between city-regions. Groupings of cities could put forward different aspects of the overall investor portfolio offering. Combining the investment offerings of different city-regions in a single broad package would provide for a more comprehensive portfolio of investment opportunities to potential investors, but this also requires alignment on the different levels of the economic development strategies of the cities which are working together.

Growth of defence industry

At the time of writing this chapter, the dramatic changes and turmoil in the international political economy of global trade and security mean that defence has once again become central to discussions of economic growth and development in a manner which has not been the case for many decades. The UK defence-related advanced manufacturing sector has assets and facilities which are widely distributed across the country's economic geography and offers an anchoring for the types of approaches outlined here. Major defence-related advanced manufacturing investments are located in Lancashire, Derbyshire, West Midlands, East Midlands, North Wales, the North-East, Yorkshire and Humber, South Wales, Kent, Bristol, Devon, Hampshire, Scotland and Northern Ireland, among others. These investments spearhead complex supply chains criss-crossing the country as well as internationally, and range across numerous technologies and sectors.

The rebuilding of the UK's defence capabilities will genuinely be a national effort, in that it cannot be focused simply on the South-East, nor can it be focused almost exclusively on the tertiary-educated workforce. A wide array of skill types will be required to rebuild the UK defence capabilities at volume, and this strategy lends itself to a much broader regional logic than simply a focus on the knowledge economy in cities and high-technology sectors. The new defence agenda will require enormous scale as well as skills and technology, and UK cities working together are well placed to provide the basis for this.

Summary

To realise the productivity growth potential associated with their economic scale, the northern cities of the UK need to be able to move increasingly in the directions of greater coordination over fragmentation, alignment over competition and genuinely devolved decision making over responses to central government directives. The Devolution White Paper of 2024 and the Industrial Strategy Green Paper of 2024 provide many pointers in these directions, but over the coming years we will need to go much further than these templates imply.

Given these challenges, it is clear that a national economic growth strategy which is based on promoting further growth in one corner of the country is never going to be meaningful in the long term. For a national growth strategy to be viable it has to include at its core serious initiatives aimed at galvanising regions which have been less prosperous, and which also engage with a much wider variety of sectors. Therefore, an industrial strategy which primarily focuses just on advanced sectors and technologies, allied with further investments in infrastructure in the South-East, will fail to galvanise much of the country, being so heavily oriented on all dimensions to the South-East. Instead, what is needed is a national growth strategy which engages with a wider range of sectors, technologies, cities and regions.

Key recommendations

- In order to foster the type and scale of investment needed to turn northern cities around, actions aimed at building scale and coordination are essential. While mayoral combined authorities are an important step in the right direction, all UK cities outside of London are still operating at below-scale ranges in comparison to peer groups of cities across the OECD. US and Japanese cities are far bigger than UK cities, and while UK cities are of similar orders of magnitude to European cities, comparator and competitor cities in other parts of Europe typically have city centre commercial districts which are two or three times bigger than those in the UK.[45]
- For attracting direct investment, both foreign and domestic, northern cities need to build scale and to coordinate their investment potential offering. As discussed here, this could be undertaken by setting up a joint investment-promotion programme in which northern and midlands city-regions pool their various resources in order to drive a wider pan-regional strategy.
- The urgent need for a heavily renewed and up-scaled defence agenda offers northern cities and regions exactly the type of scale-related challenge that coordinated activities can be designed to meet.

Notes

1 P. McCann (2024) 'Levelling up economics', *Oxford Open Economics*, 3, Special Issue, *Dimensions of Inequality: The IFS Deaton Review*: i616–i624; P. Veneri and F. Murtin (2019) 'Where are the highest living standards? Measuring well-being and inclusiveness in OECD regions', *Regional Studies*, 53: 657–66.
2 P. McCann (2016) *The UK Regional-National Economic Problem: Geography, Globalisation and Governance*, London: Routledge; McCann (2024).
3 McCann (2016).
4 McCann (2016).
5 McCann (2024).
6 P. McCann (2023) 'Levelling up UK regions: scale-related challenges of Brexit, investment and land use', *Contemporary Social Science*, 18(3–4): 298–317.
7 McCann (2016).
8 *The Independent* (1998) 'Monitor: Eddie George on unemployment. Reflections on comments by the governor of the Bank of England about the effects of high interest rates', www.independent.co.uk/arts-entertainment/monitor-eddie-george-on-unemployment-1180133.html (accessed 6 May 2025).
9 McCann (2016).
10 O-J. Blanchard and L. F. Katz (1992) 'Regional evolutions', *Brookings Papers on Economic Activity*, 1: 1–61; R. J. Barro (1997) *Determinants of Economic Growth: A Cross-Country Empirical Study*, Cambridge MA: MIT Press; R. J. Barro and X. Sala-i-Martin (1995) *Economic Growth*, Cambridge MA: MIT Press; A. Carrascal-Incera, P. McCann, R. Ortega-Argilés and A. Rodriguez-Pose (2020) 'UK interregional inequality in a historical and international comparative context', *National Institute Economic Review*, 253: R4–R17.
11 Carrascal-Incera et al. (2020).
12 McCann (2016).
13 McCann (2016); N. O'Brien and G. Miscampbell (2020, 6 March) *Levelling Up: Rebalancing Growth-enhancing Spending*, London: Onward; T. Forth and R. Jones (2020) *The Missing £4bn, Making R and D Work for the Whole UK*, London: NESTA.
14 McCann (2016).
15 HMT and DTI (2001, November) *Productivity in the UK: 3–The Regional Dimension*, London: HM Treasury and Department for Trade and Industry; HMT and ODPM (2003, July) *Productivity in the UK: 4 The Local Dimension*, London: HM Treasury and Office of the Deputy Prime Minister; NAO (2007, February) *Mind the Gap: Tackling Disparities in Regional Economic Performance*, London: National Audit Office.
16 A. Haldane (2018) 'The UK's productivity problem: hub no spokes', Speech by Andy Haldane, Academy of Social Sciences Annual Lecture, London, 28 June, www.bankofengland.co.uk/speech/2018/andy-h (accessed 6 May 2025).

17 A. Bounds (2015) 'Lure of the south too strong for northern businesses: household names have been taken over with headquarters moved overseas or to the southeast', *Financial Times*, 15 March.
18 A. Kirk (2019) 'Where are the UK's most powerful companies based? The FTSE 100 is more diverse than you think', CityAM, 7 June, www.cityam.com/north-south-divide-ftse-100-more-diverse-you-think/ (accessed 6 May 2025).
19 Bounds (2015).
20 F. Haque (2023) 'How big is the north–south divide?', Beauhurst, 1 June, www.beauhurst.com/blog/how-big-is-the-north-south-divide/ (accessed 6 May 2025).
21 C. Mayer, P. McCann and J. Schumacher (2021) 'The structure and relations of banking systems: the UK experience and the challenges of "levelling-up"', *Oxford Review of Economic Policy*, 37(1): 152–71.
22 J. Kay, M. King (2020) *Radical Uncertainty – Decision-making beyond the numbers*, New York: W. W. Norton & Company.
23 M. Daams, P. McCann, P. Veneri and R. Barkham (2024a), 'Capital shocks, the great recession, and UK regional divergence', *Regional Studies*, 58(12): 2256–75; M. Daams, C. Mayer and P. McCann (2024b), 'Regions, cities and finance: the role of capital shocks and banking reforms in shaping the UK geography of prosperity', TPI Productivity Insights Paper No. 041, Manchester: The Productivity Institute.
24 Daams et al. (2024b).
25 Daams et al. (2024a); Daams et al. (2024b).
26 Daams et al. (2024a); Daams et al. (2024b).
27 M. Daams, P. McCann, P. Veneri and R. Barkham (2025) 'Is the UK sterling-zone an optimal currency area? Comparisons with the euro area and the rest of Europe using city and regional investment data', TPI Working Paper 050, Manchester: The Productivity Institute; M. Kahn, 'UK's one-size-fits-all monetary policy doesn't work outside London', *The Times*, 10 February.
28 P. McCann and R. Ortega-Argilés (2021) 'The UK "geography of discontent": narratives, Brexit and inter-regional "levelling up"', *Cambridge Journal of Regions, Economy and Society*, 14: 545–64.
29 Carrascal-Incera et al. (2020).
30 McCann (2016).
31 S. Frick, I. Taylor, P. Prenzel, K. Penney, P. Collier, V. Goodstadt, C. Mayer and P. McCann (2023) *Lessons from Successful 'Turnaround' Cities for the UK*, The Economy 2030 Inquiry, London: Resolution Foundation, https://economy2030.resolutionfoundation.org/reports/lessons-from-successful-turnaround-cities-for-the-uk/ (accessed 6 May 2025).
32 For Haldane's wider views on productivity, skills and devolution see alliancembs.manchester.ac.uk/original-thinking-applied/magazine/issue-08/levelling-with-us/ (accessed 6 May 2025)

33 P. McCann and P-Y. Yuan (2022) 'The productivity performance of different types of UK regions and the challenges of levelling up', *National Institute Economic Review*, 261(1): 79–98.
34 A. Stansbury, D. Turner and E. Balls (2023) 'Tackling the UK's regional economic inequality: binding constraints and avenues for policy intervention', *Contemporary Social Science*, 18(3–4): 318–56; J. Burn-Murdoch (2023) 'Britain's graduates are being short-changed while America's are rich: university-level skills are in much higher and more lucrative demand in the US than the UK', *Financial Times*, 27 October.
35 McCann (2016).
36 G. Rodrigues, O. Vera and P. Swinney (2022, December) *At the Frontier: The Geography of the UK's New Economy*, London: Centre for Cities.
37 G. Rodrigues and A. Breach (2021, November) *Measuring Up: Comparing Public Transport in the UK and Europe's Biggest Cities*, London: Centre for Cities; A. Breach and P. Swinney (2024, June) *Climbing the Summit: Big Cities in the UK and the G7*, London: Centre for Cities.
38 ONS (2017, April) *Exploring Labour Productivity in Rural and Urban Areas in Great Britain: 2014*, London: Office for National Statistics; ONS (2019) 'Understanding spatial labour productivity in the UK', London: Office for National Statistics, www.ons.gov.uk/employmentandlabourmarket/peopleinwork/labourproductivity/articles/understandingspatiallabourproductivityintheuk/2019-05-03 (accessed 6 May 2025); ONS (2020) 'Understanding Towns in England and Wales: spatial analysis', London: Office for National Statistics, www.ons.gov.uk/peoplepopulationandcommunity/populationandmigration/populationestimates/datasets/understandingtownsinenglandandwalesspatialanalysis (accessed 6 May 2025).
39 McCann and Yuan (2022).
40 ONS (2017); ONS (2019); ONS (2020); McCann and Yuan (2022).
41 J-E. Garcilazo and J. Oliveira Martins (2020) 'New trends in regional policy: place-based component and structural policies', in M. Fischer and P. Nijkamp (eds) *Handbook of Regional Science*, Berlin: Springer.
42 T. Pope, G. Dalton and M. Coggins (2022, December) *Subnational Government in England: An International Comparison*, London: Institute for Government.
43 Frick et al. (2023).
44 McCann (2016); Pope et al. (2022).
45 Breach and Swinney (2024); Rodrigues and Breach (2021).

4

THE FUTURE OF FINANCE: FINANCIAL TECHNOLOGY AND INNOVATION FOR GROWTH

Catherine L. Mann* and Markos Zachariadis

Introduction

Digital innovation in financial services has been a focal point of academic and policy discussions for more than half a century.[1] Early waves of technological change included the introduction of mainframe computing in banks in the 1960s and 1970s, followed by the widespread adoption of automated teller machines (ATMs) in the 1980s and internet banking in the late 1990s.[2]

These innovations collectively laid the groundwork for more sophisticated transformations by reducing the cost of basic transactions, enhancing data processing capabilities and enabling new channels of customer engagement.[3] Over time, these foundational technologies evolved into integrated digital platforms, providing a launchpad for financial technology (FinTech) firms to disrupt and transform traditional financial processes.[4]

Accelerating digitisation

The subsequent growth of high-speed internet, mobile connectivity and cloud computing has accelerated this digitisation, with such advances empowering not only established banks but also new entrants such as challenger banks, payment start-ups and digital asset platforms,

---

* The views expressed in this chapter are Dr Mann's own and do not reflect the views of the Bank of England, the Monetary Policy Committee or staff.

all looking to expand service offerings, often at lower cost and higher speed than legacy institutions.[5]

A key outcome of these technological shifts has been 'disintermediation', namely the reduction or elimination of intermediaries in financial transactions. New platforms and FinTech solutions allow individuals and businesses to obtain credit, transfer money or invest savings without necessarily relying on large, incumbent banks.[6] However, while digital innovation has opened the financial services sector to heightened competition, thereby pressuring incumbents to adopt new technologies and revamp existing processes, the scale and success of these disruptive initiatives varies across different jurisdictions.[7]

FinTech and economic growth

In this chapter we review the evidence on the effect of FinTech and innovation adoption on economic growth and productivity in the financial services sector, with follow-on assessment for business investment and economy-wide productivity. In doing so we highlight various emerging technologies that have contributed to the transformation of the financial services industry and the various institutions within, as well as having a huge impact on the global financial system. We also discuss the increasing challenges around data and the development of open banking systems. The implications for business investment and macroeconomic productivity are nuanced and depend on to what extent and what type of innovations in financial services are accessed and used by businesses.

We conclude with a discussion about what these trends mean for business school teaching and research, and the role of schools in debates over the control and ownership of the vast information generated today through financial transactions.

The benefits and growth of ICT investment

There is now considerable evidence that information and communication technology (ICT) can yield noteworthy economic benefits at both the macroeconomic and firm level.[8] Extensive research has also highlighted the positive influence of ICT investments on multiple financial performance indicators.[9] ICT investment can also produce significant returns at an industry level. One study, for instance, examined sixty-one US industries and found that sectors leveraging ICT most intensively experienced accelerated productivity growth, as measured by both total factor productivity and average labour productivity.[10] However, while additional studies have supported these conclusions, the degree of ICT's impact varies considerably across different economies and sectors.[11] For instance, another study noted that the most pronounced effects were in information technology-heavy service sectors.[12] Firm-level studies have further reinforced the positive relationship between ICT adoption and business performance.

The financial sector has consistently been one of the largest investors in technology, perhaps because at its core it is an information business and managing information more effectively can lead to higher returns and economic gains as well as more competition. Investment data has historically confirmed this trend, with the banking, securities and insurance industries accounting for a significant share of global ICT spend.

Effects on the global financial system

Such widespread adoption of ICT has had profound implications for the global financial system, not only in terms of transforming transaction processing but also in reshaping organisational and market structures.[13] It has also led to the emergence of novel financial products and altered workplace dynamics.[14] And it has facilitated the wider globalisation of financial markets.[15]

Over the years, various studies have analysed ICT's specific impact on the economic performance of financial institutions. For instance, one study used a dataset of nearly 7,000 banks in twenty-nine countries in Europe and the Americas to examine the effect of the SWIFT payment network on bank performance.[16] It found that the network had large effects on profitability in the long term and significant network effects on performance. Another study examined the impact of information technology (IT) adoption on bank performance during the initial stages of the COVID-19 pandemic.[17] Those results showed that high IT adopters performed better in terms of market returns while, significantly, the study also showed that technology adoption fosters banks' ability to withstand economic downturns, ultimately contributing to greater financial stability.

A number of studies have also focused on how technology can affect business models as well as industry architecture and competition in financial services. For instance, one study examined how technology standards in the UK banking sector – that were largely imposed via Open Banking regulations in 2018 – shifted the architecture of the industry through the emergence of new institutions that brokered data connectivity between banks and third-party providers.[18]

The data debate

As ICT is ever more adopted in financial services, so data has unsurprisingly become of increasing strategic significance in financial services. Debates over the control and ownership of the vast information generated through financial transactions have also intensified. In particular, a critical question arises. Should financial institutions or consumers have authority over this data? The resolution of this issue will significantly influence market competition, technological investment and overall industry dynamics. Given that data is an essential asset for enhancing efficiency, refining risk assessment and driving innovation, financial institutions stand to gain a competitive edge through superior data access, enabling more precise pricing, targeted customer segmentation and reduced operational costs. However, when traditional banking entities monopolise data, this can create barriers to competition and diminishes consumer benefits.[19]

One of the most promising approaches to addressing this challenge is the concept of data portability, which has gained widespread recognition for its potential to empower consumers.[20] In essence, data portability grants individuals control over their financial data and the ability to share it securely with authorised third-party providers, thereby fostering a more competitive financial ecosystem. As such, open banking initiatives, which facilitate seamless data sharing between financial institutions and external service providers, have begun to take shape across various economies.

This shift towards open banking, and to an extent open finance, is expected to enhance market efficiency by fostering competition, spurring innovation and improving financial inclusion.[21] It is particularly beneficial for 'underserved' populations such as small businesses and individuals who have historically faced barriers to traditional banking services. By enabling secure and transparent data exchanges, open banking can lead to the creation of more affordable and tailored financial products, ultimately improving consumer access and financial wellbeing.

Financial services, business investment and productivity growth

Innovations in financial institutions can affect productivity growth through several channels. Directly, by raising productivity growth in financial institutions and the financial sector, productivity growth in the economy increases according to the weight of the sector in the economy. For the UK, where the financial sector represents some 10 per cent of output, this arithmetic gain to overall productivity growth could be notable.

More broadly, however, it is how innovation in the financial sector influences the productivity growth of *users* of financial services that matters. Analogous to the productivity gains associated with widespread use of ICT, rather than the productivity gains within the ICT sector itself we need to consider ways in which innovations in financial services could affect productivity growth throughout the economy. One lens is to consider how business investment and productivity might be affected by the innovations in financial institutions and services.

Business investment backdrop[22]

Before looking specifically at these links, however, it is worth first reviewing the state of business investment in the UK. That UK business investment has underperformed is not a new observation. By various assessments, UK business investment has been weak for decades, was particularly sluggish after the global financial crisis and has slowed further since Brexit and COVID-19. Slow global demand growth, reduced competitive pressures, higher uncertainty of various types, financial constraints facing firms, underexploited agglomeration and network externalities, inequalities of place and rising earnings management are variously cited as culprits holding back business investment. Some of these headwinds are more prevalent in the UK, and a question for research is whether innovations within financial institutions could moderate or accentuate those headwinds.

Drivers of business investment

There are three different perspectives on what drives business investment – the cost of capital, managerial decision making and financial investors. Innovation in financial services can play an important role in each of these areas.

A standard economist's equation for business investment is based on the cost of capital and market sales. In this regard the evidence suggests that the cost of capital matters relatively more for smaller firms, young and fast-growing firms and firms with less liquidity buffers.[23] So, innovations in financial services that extend to these firms could be particularly relevant.

But for many firms it is not the external cost of capital (which is what the financial sector provides) that matters most for business investment but, rather, an internal 'hurdle' rate – the minimum rate of return on an investment that will offset its costs. In a 2016 survey, the average hurdle rate across UK businesses was 12 per cent, substantially higher than the calculated cost of capital (which is derived from the cost of debt and equity) at around 6.5 per cent.[24] The wedge for small firms was larger, suggesting those managers have a higher degree of risk aversion to accessing borrowing. Innovations in financial services or relationship building between financial services providers and smaller firms could raise business investment. Also, even though the hurdle rate dominates a direct measure of the financial cost of capital (such as the weighted average cost of capital calculated from debt and equity costs), research using earnings calls for US firms shows that the gap between the hurdle rate and the financial cost of capital matters.[25]

Competitive pressures

Firms facing competitive pressures appear to undertake more business investment to keep their competitive edge, including through innovative R&D.[26] Since intangibles – including R&D, databases and software – are harder to value, these types of investments are less likely to be used as collateral, so are less supported by external finance.[27] Indeed, one study has shown that investment in intangibles is positively associated with higher internal cash flow, especially for large, young and private firms, but not for public firms.[28] Because public firms have greater transparency of accounts and attention from analysts, this seems to moderate the valuation challenge of intangibles so that these firms need to depend less on internal cash flow for intangibles investment.

Cash flow earnings can be deployed for business investment, or for financial investment such as mergers and acquisitions (M&A), or returned to shareholders (including managers) via stock buybacks and dividends. If the return, or perceived return, to any of these financial investments exceeds that of business investment – for whatever reason associated with cost of capital or time horizon or managerial or institutional objectives – then deploying earnings for financial investments would take precedence over business investment. Research using

UK data shows that business investment is negatively correlated with a high share of financial investment within a business.[29]

The role of financial institutions

The important point here in terms of our wider discussion is that financial institutions such as banks can help to reduce the cost of capital via their role as information gatherers that assess management quality and investment decisions. By building relationships, financial institutions can improve decision making by owners, increasing the likelihood that profitable investments will be undertaken. Financial innovation, particularly with regard to creditworthiness, can aid both the borrower and the lender. However, as the concentration of financial institutions increases – such as by institutional investors as shareholders – the boundary between the investor and the firm can blur. Business investment decisions may be driven by the institutions' objectives, cost of capital and assessment of market prospects. Research finds that the more concentrated are the financial investors, the less business investment is undertaken, with knock-on effects on productivity.[30]

It is relevant to note here that less than half of 1 per cent of all UK firms account for more than half of all UK business investment. These firms are subsidiaries of multinationals, which have been stable leaders in the UK marketplace since 2010.[31] Meanwhile, institutional investors account for 60 per cent of market capitalisation, split about half-and-half into foreign and domestic institutional investors. The top three institutional investors own about 23 per cent of each of the listed firms in the UK.[32] Hence, the issue of concentration in the provision of financial services, and the potential for financial innovation to affect that concentration, matters.

In the UK one institutional investor and the evolution of its portfolio stands out, namely pension funds. In 2008 pension schemes invested about two-thirds of their assets under management into equities and property, with about a quarter of their assets held in UK company stock shares. By 2022 about a third was invested in equities and property and only 2 per cent in UK stock shares. The shift has been toward bonds, particularly UK gilts. Pension fund regulation may interact with financial institutions and appear to affect how cash flow is deployed. Firms making their own decisions, and faced with pension deficits, paid lower dividends but kept up their business investment programmes. Firms that made non-voluntary contributions to the regulator reduced both dividends and business investment, the more so if the firms faced financial constraints.[33]

The role of managers

Managers ultimately decide on whether to undertake business investment. In this regard, researchers have looked at the relationship between earnings reporting and firm performance, including business investment. The UK required mandatory quarterly reporting in 2014 and then dropped that requirement in 2017, though one study suggests that the reporting requirement (or lack thereof) did not affect business investment.[34] However, following the requirement to report, firms did give more qualitative views of current performance and guidance on future objectives. More analysts covered these reports, and accuracy of future prospects improved. When reporting was no longer mandatory, only 10 per cent of firms chose to stop reporting, mostly smaller firms, and analyst coverage of those firms fell.

Policy variability, such as the frequent changes in capital tax credits, appears to take a toll on business investment too.[35] For instance, another study has reported how heightened economic uncertainty is associated with managers holding a larger cash buffer.[36]

To summarise, the way in which financial services affects business investment is an important ingredient in productivity growth. As we discuss above, financial services can influence the cost and availability of capital, for example for smaller or younger firms, or for intangible, harder-to-collateralise investment. Innovation in financial services provisions to consumers could also affect business investment by affecting housing mortgage terms to support consumer demand, a key driver of business investment.

However, some innovations in financial services might not yield increased business investment and productivity growth. Innovations to M&A and equity buybacks, for example, may be advantageous for the firm's managers or stockholders, but not necessarily for productivity-enhancing business investment.

The modern productivity paradox

Despite the great potential of technologies and past evidence that show a positive effect on firm outcomes from earlier ICT adoption, there is little evidence that highlights a sustained and significant effect of technology on aggregate productivity statistics.[37] For instance, in the US, aggregate labour productivity growth averaged only 1.3 per cent per year from 2005 to 2016 (which is less than half of the 2.8 per cent annual growth rate reported from 1995 to 2004). OECD countries saw very similar decelerations.

Brynjolfsson et al.'s paper on *Artificial Intelligence and the Modern Productivity Paradox* discusses a few reasons why this might be the case.[38] The authors argue that the biggest contributor is long implementation (and restructuring) lags, especially for advanced technologies that take time to adopt and combine with more complementary innovations. However, technologies can still potentially combine to generate evident accelerations in aggregate productivity growth.

For instance, a very recent study on generative AI at work found that access to generative AI assistants dramatically increased worker productivity, by 14 per cent on average, in a sample of customer support agents.[39] A similar study by The Productivity Institute also found that technological solutions can be utilised by chief financial officers as productivity-enhancing mechanisms to boost the business performance of their organisation.[40] More specifically, adopting advanced data solutions like data lakes can enhance data accuracy, enable real-time reporting and streamline decision making. Automating data processes has the potential to also reduce reliance on manual corrections, saving time and improving efficiency. Such systems can also facilitate access to reliable, detailed insights, ensuring informed evaluations of marketing and workforce strategies. However, implementing such technology demands expertise in data science, a skill often lacking among finance professionals. To bridge this gap, companies can establish centres of excellence, bringing in data specialists and fostering collaboration between finance and IT departments.

As can therefore be seen, achieving consensus regarding the magnitude and nature of the benefits from ICT remains elusive and depends on the context of the business or industry as well as the technology in play.

Summary

The digital transformation of financial services has evolved dramatically and FinTech has played a significant role in economic growth and productivity, impacting on both traditional institutions and emerging competitors. The financial sector remains a major investor in ICT, with banking and securities leading global technology spending. Studies show that ICT investment enhances efficiency, profitability and market competitiveness, with digital platforms reshaping financial transactions, organisational structures and global market integration.

The growing importance of data in financial services has intensified debates over data control and ownership. Open banking and data portability initiatives have emerged to increase competition, innovation and financial inclusion by enabling secure sharing of financial information. However, concerns remain over market concentration and consumer benefits.

The financial sector also influences business investment and productivity. However, financial innovation does not always lead to productivity growth, as activities like mergers, acquisitions and stock buybacks can prioritise shareholder returns over business expansion. Despite the potential of new technologies, their impact on overall productivity remains debated. Long adoption lags and skill shortages hinder immediate gains. However, AI and data-driven financial tools show promise in enhancing efficiency, decision making and competitive advantage in financial services.

Key recommendations

Universities, and more specifically business schools, can play a vital role in ensuring more concrete and positive results when it comes to technological and other innovation applications in financial services.

- Firstly, more research can be developed to examine the specificities of emerging technologies (and other innovations) and how these can contribute to the growth of the sector as well as the labour productivity of the workforce within. For example, how can generative AI, distributed ledgers or smart data lead to novel and more accessible financial services, or increase the access to borrowing for SMEs? These are some of the questions being looked at right now by the Centre for Financial Technology Studies at AMBS.
- Secondly, business schools are well positioned to 'upskill' and 'reskill' the workforce in order to tackle technological developments more effectively and learn how to utilise these for business growth and increased productivity. Such digital leadership and innovation management skills will also lead to smaller lags in implementing advanced technologies and restructuring organisations, while at the same time exploring complementarities with other innovations and recombining with business processes.[41]

Notes

1. E. Rizopoulos and M. Zachariadis (2024) 'Fintech's impact on the banking industry and financial services', in H. K. Baker, G. Filbeck and K. Black (eds) *The Emerald Handbook of Fintech: Reshaping Finance*, Bingley: Emerald Publishing Limited.
2. B. Bátiz-Lazo (2009) 'Emergence and evolution of ATM networks in the UK, 1967–2000', *Business History*, 51(1): 1–27, https://doi.org/10.1080/00076790802602164

3   S. V. Scott and M. Zachariadis (2012) 'Origins and development of SWIFT, 1973–2009', *Business History*, 54(3): 462–82, https://doi.org/10.1080/00076791.2011.638502
4   V. Murinde, E. Rizopoulos and M. Zachariadis (2022) 'The impact of the FinTech revolution on the future of banking: opportunities and risks', *International Review of Financial Analysis*, 81, 102103, https://doi.org/10.1016/j.irfa.2022.102103
5   M. Zachariadis (2020) 'Data-sharing frameworks in financial services: discussing open banking regulation for Canada', SSRN, https://dx.doi.org/10.2139/ssrn.2983066; M. Zachariadis (2025) 'Data portability in financial services: a research note on the progress and debates around Canadian open banking regulation', *Global Risk Institute Paper Series*, https://dx.doi.org/10.2139/ssrn.5129284
6   CMA (2016) *Making banks work harder for customers*, www.gov.uk/government/uploads/system/uploads/attachment_data/file/544942/overview-of-the-banking-retail-market.pdf (accessed 20 February 2018).
7   Bank of England and Financial Conduct Authority (2024) *Artificial Intelligence in UK Financial Services – 2024*, www.bankofengland.co.uk/report/2024/artificial-intelligence-in-uk-financial-services-2024 (accessed 6 May 2025)..
8   E. Brynjolfsson (1993) 'The productivity paradox of information technology', *Communications of the ACM*, 36(12): 66–77; N. Bloom, R. Sadun and J. Van Reenen (2012) 'Americans do IT better: US multinationals and the productivity miracle', *American Economic Review*, 102(1): 167–201.
9   S. Aral, E. Brynjolfsson and D. J. Wu (2006) 'Which came first, IT or productivity? The virtuous cycle of investment and use in enterprise systems', in *Proceedings of the 27th International Conference on Information Systems*, Milwaukee, pp. 1–22; T. F. Bresnahan, E. Brynjolfsson and L. M. Hitt (2002) 'Information technology, workplace organization and the demand for skilled labor', *Quarterly Journal of Economics*, 117(1): 339–76; E. Brynjolfsson and L. M. Hitt (1996) 'Paradox lost? Firm-level evidence on the returns to information systems spending', *Management Science*, 42(4): 541–58; E. Brynjolfsson and L. M. Hitt (2000) 'Beyond computation: information technology, organizational transformation and business performance', *Journal of Economic Perspectives*, 14(4): 23–48; E. Brynjolfsson and L. M. Hitt (2003) 'Computing productivity: firm-level evidence', *The Review of Economics and Statistics*, 85(4): 793–808; S. Dewan and K. L. Kraemer (2000) 'Information technology and productivity: evidence from country-level data', *Management Science*, 46(4): 548–62.
10 K. Stiroh (2002) 'Information technology and the US productivity revival: what do the industry data say?' *American Economic Review*, 92(5): 1559–76; W. Wang, F. F. Moreira and Y. Liang (2024) 'Does FinTech adoption improve bank performance?' *International Journal of Monetary Economics and Finance*, 1–28, https://doi.org/10.1504/IJMEF.2023.10058590
11 D. Siegel and Z Griliches (1992) 'Purchased services, outsourcing, computers, and productivity in manufacturing', in Zvi Griliches (ed.) *Output Measurement in the Service Sectors*, Cambridge MA: National Bureau of Economic Research,

Inc., pp. 429–60; E. R. Berndt and C. J. Morrison (1995) 'High-tech capital formation and economic performance in U.S. manufacturing industries: an exploratory analysis', *Journal of Econometrics*, 65: 9–43.
12 Stiroh (2002); Wang et al. (2024).
13 D. Dinçkol, P. Ozcan and M. Zachariadis (2023) 'Regulatory standards and consequences for industry architecture: the case of UK open banking', *Research Policy*, Elsevier, 52(6): 104760; S. V. Scott and G. Walsham (1998) 'Shifting boundaries and new technologies: a case study in the UK banking sector', in *Proceedings of the International Conference of Information Systems*, Helsinki, Finland, pp. 177–87.
14 M. Barrett and G. Walsham (1999) 'Electronic trading and work transformation in the London insurance market', *Information Systems Research*, 10(1): 1–22.
15 S. Sassen (2002) *Global Networks, Linked Cities*, London: Routledge; B. W. Weber, (1994) 'Information technology in the major international financial Markets', in C. P. Deans and K. R. Karwan (eds) *Global Information Systems and Technology: Focus on the Organization and Its Functional Areas*, Hershey PA: IGI Publishing, pp. 132–66.
16 S. V. Scott, J. Van Reenen and M. Zachariadis (2017) 'The long-term effect of digital innovation on bank performance: an empirical study of SWIFT adoption in financial services', *Research Policy*, 46(5), 984–1004.
17 A. Dadoukis, M. Fiaschetti and G. Fusi (2021) 'IT adoption and bank performance during the Covid-19 pandemic', *Economics Letters*, 204, 109904, https://doi.org/10.1016/j.econlet.2021.109904
18 Dinçkol et al. (2023).
19 Zachariadis (2025).
20 Zachariadis (2020).
21 Dinçkol et al. (2023)
22 This section draws on C. L. Mann (2024) *UK Business Investment: Economists, Managers, Financiers. An Integrated Framework to Analyse the Past and Underpin Prospects*, Productivity Insights Paper No. 036, The Productivity Institute, www.productivity.ac.uk/wp-content/uploads/2024/06/PIP036-Business-Investment-FINAL-180624.pdf (accessed 23 April 2025).
23 A. Carella, R. Chen and X. Shao (2023) *Enhancing Business Investment in the United Kingdom*, Washington, DC: International Monetary Fund; Dang (research in process, AMBS, 2025); Xue and Mann (research in process, AMBS, 2025).
24 M. Melolinna, H. Miller and S. Tatomir (2018) *Business Investment, Cost of Capital and Uncertainty in the United Kingdom – Evidence from Firm-level Analysis*, Working Paper No. 717, London: Bank of England.
25 N. J. Gormsen and K. Huber (2023) *Corporate Discount Rates*, NBER Working Paper 31329, Cambridge MA: National Bureau of Economic Research, Inc.
26 G. Gutierrez and T. Philippon (2018) 'Ownership, concentration, and investment', *AEA Papers and Proceedings*, 108: 432–37.
27 For the UK, the Office for National Statistics defines intangibles as: 'Intangible assets include products such as software and databases, research and development

(R&D), mineral exploration, and artistic originals, as recorded in the UK National Accounts (capitalised). These are collectively referred to as intellectual property products (IPP). However, there is an additional set of intangible assets, such as branding, financial product innovation, firm-specific training, and design, that are not included in the UK National Accounts. These are referred to as "uncapitalised intangible assets".'

28 E. Adu-Ameyaw, A. Danso, M. Uddin and S. Acheampong (2022) 'Investment-cash flow sensitivity: evidence from investment in identifiable intangible and tangible assets activities'. *International Journal of Finance & Economics*, 29(2): 1179–204, https://doi.org/10.1002/ijfe.2730.

29 D. Tori and Ö. Onaran (2018) 'The effects of financialization on investment: evidence from firm-level data for the UK', *Cambridge Journal of Economics* 42(5): 1393–416.

30 M. Hadani, M. Goranova and R. Khan (2010) 'Institutional investors, shareholder activism, and earnings management', *Journal of Business Research* 64(12): 1352–36. See also N. Choi, M. Fedenia, H. Skiba and T. Sokolyk (2017) 'Portfolio concentration and performance of institutional investors worldwide', *Journal of Financial Economics 123*(1): 189–08; T. Hanappi, V. Millot and S. Turban (2023) 'How does corporate taxation affect business investment? Evidence from aggregate and firm-level data (No. 1765)', Paris: *OECD Publishing*.

31 Hanappi et al. (2023).

32 A. Medina, A. de la Cruz and Y. Tang (2022) 'Corporate ownership and concentration (No. 27)', Paris: *OECD Publishing*.

33 P. Bunn, P. Mizen and P. Smietanka (2018) 'Growing pension deficits and the expenditure decisions of UK companies', Discussion Papers 2018/05, University of Nottingham, Centre for Finance, Credit and Macroeconomics (CFCM).

34 R. C. Pozen, S. Nallareddy and S. Rajgopal (2017) 'Impact of reporting frequency on UK public companies', Charlottesville VA: CFA Institute Research Foundation.

35 D. Coyle (2023) 'Long-term perspectives and large-scale investments', www.productivity.ac.uk/news/diane-coyle-at-the-treasury-committee-long-term-perspectives-and-large-scale-investments/ (accessed 17 March 2025).

36 P. Smietanka, N. Bloom and P. Mizen (2018) *Business Investment, Cash Holding and Uncertainty since the Great Financial Crisis*, Staff Working Paper No. 753, London: Bank of England.

37 E. Brynjolfsson, D. Rock and C. Syverson (2017) *Artificial Intelligence and the Modern Productivity Paradox: A Clash of Expectations and Statistics*, NBER Working Paper 24001, Cambridge MA: National Bureau of Economic Research, Inc.

38 Brynjolfsson et al. (2017).

39 E. Brynjolfsson, D. Li and L. Raymond (2025) 'Generative AI at work', *The Quarterly Journal of Economics*, 140(2): 899–942, https://doi.org/10.1093/qje/qjae044

40 I. Teneva (AICPA-CIMA) and B. van Ark (The Productivity Institute) (2024) *Unlocking Productivity: Collaborative Synergies for Chief Financial Officers*, Strategic Productivity Series, Manchester: The Productivity Institute.
41 AMBS's Master's programme in Digital Transformation and Financial Technology pathway) was designed for exactly this purpose, namely to train the next generation of digital leaders in financial services and beyond.

5

THE IMPORTANCE OF MANAGEMENT AND LEADERSHIP FOR BETTER WELLBEING AND PRODUCTIVITY IN THE WORKPLACE

Cary Cooper and Tera Allas

Introduction: the increasing mental health problem

Latest figures from the Health and Safety Executive make for grave reading.[1] Data from 2023/24 showed that nearly 50 per cent of the cases of work-related ill-health were attributed to stress, depression and anxiety.[2] Some 776,000 workers reported suffering from these conditions, costing 16.4 million working days. Specific sectors such as public administration, defence, human health and social work have particularly high rates, some almost double the all-industries average. Evidence of the mental health crisis can also be found in other statistics. Meanwhile, although levels of musculoskeletal disorders are still high in the UK (548,000 in 2023/24), the figures are gradually coming down as employers learn to manage such disorders better. The opposite seems to be happening with mental health.

Yet these issues around mental health aren't new. For instance, a review into workplace mental health in 2017 found that 300,000 people with long-term mental health problems lose their jobs each year, a much higher rate than those with physical conditions.[3] The report also found that many employers recognised that they were missing opportunities to intervene when employees were struggling, as there was a perceived stigma around disclosing mental health conditions. Furthermore, many of these figures – focused on absence from work – significantly underplay the size of the problem. What about the thirty-three million people 'present' at their workplaces?[4] Around 60 per cent of employees experience anxiety, and 33 per cent say their job makes them feel worried or depressed some, most or all of the time.[5] That is more than ten million people in the UK saying work is affecting their mental health. So, what is going on here? How can one begin to explain the epidemic of stress, depression and anxiety we are seeing in the British workplace, and what can be done about it?

Factors that can affect stress

Let us start by looking at the actual factors that can lead to work-related stress – and there are a multitude of them, both structural and behavioural. Structural reasons include unhappiness with your role within an organisation, lack of role clarity or autonomy, work overload or limited career development opportunities. A poor physical environment – including during the commute – can be a trigger too, as can an ineffective hybrid model, or having to use digital tools that either don't work well or which require excessive repetitive work. A mismatch between a worker's skills and aspirations and day-to-day tasks can be a key source of discontent. In a recent OECD analysis, 37 per cent of working adults in the UK said they were over-qualified for their role, the highest proportion in any of the thirty-one countries covered in the study.[6] Being over-qualified was associated with a significant reduction in life satisfaction, a good measure of someone's general wellbeing. Moreover, the National Foundation for Educational Research found that 14 per cent of UK workers feel their essential skills are significantly under-utilised, and that this was particularly widespread among lower-paid occupations.[7]

But cultural and behavioural issues are at least as important. The McKinsey Health Institute has found that one of the leading causes of burn-out is a toxic workplace, where employees don't feel supported, respected or included.[8] Poor relationships with colleagues, lack of appreciation, microaggressions or bullying are all contributors to work-related ill-health. Another factor could be 'technostress' and having to work in an 'always-on' digital culture. Symptoms of stress are played out at both the individual and organisational level. Personal symptoms include depressed mood, social isolation, poor concentration, tiredness, excessive drinking, irritability, chest pains and high blood pressure. The warning signs within an organisation include high absenteeism, high labour turnover, poor quality control, lack of innovation, lack of collaboration, poor productivity and poor customer service.

The implications of poor mental health for business performance

At an individual level poor mental health is a tragedy, a huge burden on a person's wellbeing and their ability to have a meaningful life. At the organisational level, the effects directly translate to worse business performance. The visible impacts – in the form of sick days, absenteeism or high staff turnover – are well documented. In the UK, those who say work makes them worried or depressed are three times as likely as those without these issues to say that work has made them ill.[9] And employees with low job-related wellbeing are 2.4 times as likely to want to quit their job than those with high job-related wellbeing.[10] Moreover, the less visible impacts, such as lower innovation potential, poorer collaboration, lack of personal productivity or poor customer service, are just as important. In the UK, 24 per cent of all employed people said emotional problems meant they had accomplished less than they would like, and 19 per cent said emotional problems made them work less carefully.[11] A recent study estimated the cost of worker disengagement resulting in these poor outcomes at around 4 per cent of the wage bill for an average large corporation. There is also persuasive academic evidence showing a link between engaged and happy employees and fewer sick days, higher productivity, enhanced creativity and positive workplace relationships.[12] The reverse is true for workplaces where poor mental health, stress and anxiety are highly prevalent.

Businesses are not addressing the causes of poor mental health head on

Businesses have not realised the most important lever at their disposal – line managers' skills and behaviours. Since the mid-2000s there has been a much-increased understanding about the importance of the 'healthy workplace' both to prevent work-related ill health and to help people recovering from illness or injury to return to work. At the same time, research has consistently highlighted the crucial role of management quality in driving workers' day-to-day productivity.[13] The wealth of literature comes back time and again to the importance of the line manager and, specifically, two aspects that they directly control. Firstly, good work organisation – providing workers with the context, guidance, tools and autonomy to minimise frustration and make their jobs meaningful. And secondly, psychological safety – the absence of interpersonal fear as a driver of employee behaviour.

As the primary architects of work structures and employee experiences, line managers are now the single most important driver of workplace wellbeing and productivity. Their ability to allocate resources, shape work and interact with employees can either enhance or diminish mental wellbeing. Yet, despite the recent emphasis on organisational productivity and business performance, line managers remain an overlooked factor in addressing the so-called 'productivity puzzle'. Strengthening their capabilities not only reduces sickness and ill-health at work but also improves performance, confidence and resilience in the face of economic challenges.

Sources of stress

Many of the factors that affect stress can be linked back to the line manager because they control workload, hours of work, work–life balance and career development, while they are also key in the delivery and implementation of human resources (HR) policies and practices. They also control flexible and hybrid working arrangements and have a big part to play in the extent to which everyday work spills over into everyday life, and vice versa. And, of course, line managers set the tone for an organisation's culture and behaviours. In fact, line managers are involved in all stages of an employee's journey through an organisation, from recruitment, inductions, work allocation, target setting, assessing and managing performance, through to managing health and wellbeing. A manager's style of communication and the degree to which they show support, appreciation and caring are hugely consequential for individual workers' wellbeing.

In this context it is hardly surprising that a trusting relationship with the line manager is the single most important relationship in the workplace. If workplaces are to become more resilient and agile to respond to both internal and external pressures, then line managers have a huge role in helping organisations to adapt and function in these uncertain times. Yet remarkably little attention is given in businesses to who line managers are, what they do and how they could or should be helped to undertake this important role.

The good line manager is someone employees are able to open up to and have those difficult work and personal conversations with. They are also someone who can help develop, encourage and inspire employees, unlocking and encouraging an employee's productive capacity in the workplace. By contrast, bad managers can quickly douse and stifle employee growth and engagement for even the most motivated of employees, and can have a negative impact on employee mental health and wellbeing. Sadly, the old adage that people 'join an organisation but leave a manager' still seems to ring true.

Bandwidth

If managers have constrained bandwidth, the management of employee health and wellbeing can go under the radar too. That's why it is also important that organisations look after the wellbeing of managers themselves. One challenge here is that line management responsibilities have expanded beyond traditional supervisory roles, and line managers are involved in both the implementation and delivery of HR practices and people management. Another is the changing nature of how we are working post-pandemic, because major changes in working patterns and routines can affect both employee and manager mental health too. For instance, managers should be aware that for some employees hybrid working could be really beneficial for health and wellbeing, as it can provide them with greater autonomy and control in how they work. However, depending on individual circumstances, this may not always be the case, and hybrid work could have negative unintended consequences such as the blurring of work–life boundaries.

In many respects the mental health crisis we see runs counter to the wider societal drive by companies to make working conditions more attractive and sustainable. Many boast flexible hours, good benefits and higher pay. Yet data shows that employee psychological needs are typically still going unmet, particularly for lower-earning employees, and most jobs could be enhanced to provide a much greater degree of psychological satisfaction.[14]

Recent analysis into the reasons why employees post-pandemic were leaving their jobs in record numbers (often referred to as the 'great resignation') showed that the most important factors were social and psychological, including not feeling valued by their organisation or manager, or not having a sense of belonging at work.[15]

In contrast, people at organisations with good employee–manager relations reported significantly higher satisfaction with their jobs.[16] Employees who said they had a very good relationship with their manager were five times more likely to say that they were 'very satisfied' or 'completely satisfied' with their job than employees with a very bad relationship. What is clear is that great organisations nurture good managers who instil a sense of trust and confidence, with a clear set of attainable goals rooted in customer-centric thinking. In such an environment front-line workers feel empowered and often receive positive feedback from customers and colleagues. They are also more likely to raise issues when things do not go well.

Despite the importance of people skills, managers tend to be promoted based on their technical skills

Because of the connection between happiness at work and overall life satisfaction, improving employee wellbeing could make a material difference to billions of workers, boost profitability and enhance organisational health. But, despite the huge importance of the role of the line manager, and their ability to inspire workers, in most businesses they still tend to be promoted based on their technical skills. Being a good boss isn't easy and only a small minority of people naturally have all the traits needed to be a good manager. But many incentives for leaders are also misaligned, with research suggesting that some leaders may even achieve their positions by being self-centred, overconfident, narcissistic and manipulative. By contrast, the fundamental elements of good employee–manager relations are the same as with any other human relationship – mutual trust, encouragement, empathy and good communication. In this context, it is concerning that in most functions it is common to promote people with the best technical skills rather than the best people skills. A recent study found that higher-performing salespeople were 15 per cent more likely to get promoted.[17] However, it also found that the better the salesperson's original sales performance, the *worse* the performance of their team after promotion.

Wider pressures

A complication here is that today's business leaders have never been under so much pressure, and promoting leaders with strong emotional intelligence could be regarded as a 'nice to have'. In the present economic environment shareholders are calling for foresight, bold strategies, agility and resilience, while governments and communities increasingly expect businesses to support broader goals, such as sustainability and social justice. For purpose-led corporations this is a defining moment. How can they remain committed to additional stakeholder values when the imperative is to conserve cash and, in many cases, aggressively restructure? And what about businesses that have only started defining their environmental, social and governance (ESG) ambitions? When push comes to shove, do their leaders (and shareholders) really believe in the ESG premium and, if so, where can they best focus their attention?

How to become a better manager

Despite these pressures, there are small changes individual managers can make even if their organisation has not yet made high-quality managerial relationships and worker wellbeing a systematic priority.

Firstly, a manager who genuinely cares about an employee's wellbeing tends to be curious about it. Sincerely asking 'how are you doing today?' creates an opportunity for employees to raise issues and to feel safe when they do. Secondly, the simple act of thanking people is a win-win. It doesn't cost anything, and everyone feels better. Being thanked makes people feel valued. Celebrating small achievements helps people face larger challenges and sets up a positive dynamic where everyone wants to do better. Thirdly, giving positive feedback builds employee confidence and reinforces beneficial behaviours, such as taking initiative and continuous learning. And finally, leaders must first help themselves before they can do the same for others. When highly stressed or anxious, it's hard to be empathetic, thankful and positive. Yet, more than 50 per cent of managers, directors and senior officials in the UK report that work has a negative effect on their mood at least some of the time.[18] It is only human that such pressures diminish managers' ability to support employee wellbeing.

The need to elevate workplace wellbeing and the quality of line management to the board level

To reduce absenteeism and staff turnover, and to improve productivity, businesses need to elevate workplace wellbeing and the quality of line management to board-level issues, and then monitor relentlessly.

It shouldn't just be down to individual managers to do their best to improve workplace wellbeing. Senior leaders could create a step change in both shareholder and social value by clearly articulating the sizable upsides to high psychological safety and wellbeing, including educating managers on their pivotal roles and embedding quality of workplace relationships into manager development and performance appraisals. Put simply, businesses need to start recruiting, promoting and appointing managers, and evaluating managers, based on their skills in allocating resources, structuring work, supporting team members and on their kindness, empathy, unconditional positive regard and other components of emotional intelligence. In addition, if an organisation is to really change, then it needs to move in a more strategic way and ensure it changes its culture within. We believe there are four specific steps organisations can take.

Create wellbeing metrics

Decide what good looks like. These can include both objective metrics (such as stress/mental health-related sickness absence and labour turnover) and subjective metrics (life satisfaction, job satisfaction, emotionally intelligent line manager, manageable workloads and deadlines). Metrics can also be developed in real time (such as by using apps to carry out regular stress audits, providing regular feedback on how employees feel at work). It is essential that everyone in an organisation is involved, and feedback has to be extensive. Build on existing staff surveys to get at root causes of poor workplace wellbeing.

Create a director of health and wellbeing

Reporting directly to the organisation's HR director or chief medical officer, this person should be responsible for assessing the wellbeing metrics on a regular basis and intervening where appropriate to deal with significant issues. They also develop an organisational strategy, assess line managers and look at whether flexible and hybrid work arrangements are successful. They look at the prevalence of technostress within the organisation. By having a dedicated person focused on wellbeing, an organisation can not only resolve specific issues that arise but, over time, systematically put in place processes and behaviours that become self-sustaining in creating a positive wellbeing culture.

Appoint a board member who is responsible for employee health and wellbeing

This should be someone well versed in not just the causes but also the consequences of poor wellbeing, so that they can articulate to the entire board the shareholder and stakeholder imperative of addressing the issues. Ideally, they would also have experience of implementing positive practices in other organisations, so that they can use examples from elsewhere to illustrate the positive effects of successfully managing worker wellbeing.

Consider publishing metrics in the annual report

Put the most salient wellbeing metrics in the annual report so that all stakeholders can see them. This would create a strong incentive to improve and could create a basis for broader benchmarking and best practice sharing.

In contrast to best practices, established practices tend to favour the status quo

There are costs and risks associated with the actions above. For instance, it cannot be proven in advance that creating wellbeing metrics, creating a director of wellbeing, appointing a board-level executive responsible for employee wellbeing and publishing key metrics will have only positive consequences. As is true for so many ideas, *how* these are implemented is as crucial as *what* is put in place. For example, if the metrics being covered are biased or misleading, they will not help businesses to simultaneously improve wellbeing and performance. Or, if the people appointed to key roles don't have the experience to deeply understand their organisation's situation and make pragmatic suggestions for improvement, they may end up being a drag on performance. Perhaps most challenging of all, publishing wellbeing information to the outside world is not standard in most organisations. Business leaders and board members may legitimately worry that it could be misinterpreted or taken out of context.

These risks can be mitigated, however. Published metrics can be accompanied with a clear diagnostic of causes of poor wellbeing (not all of which will be attributable to the organisation itself) and a clear narrative of how issues are responded to. They can also be put in the context of similar metrics in other organisations in the sector or in the broader population.

Towards mandatory metrics?

Even with the risk mitigations, publishing wellbeing information is likely to meet resistance. Given these challenges, should organisations be mandated to provide metrics such as job satisfaction rates, staff turnover, mental ill-health statistics and long-term sickness absence in their annual reports? Proponents would argue that mandating organisations to reveal this information could only be a good thing, especially in terms of attracting talent. Young professionals starting out on their careers would be able to see at first hand how a business or organisation is performing against a range of clearly defined wellbeing metrics. And if they don't like what they see, they won't join the organisation in the first place.

Like with any metrics, interpreting them with confidence takes time and practice. By creating an expectation of requiring published data in the future, regulators could encourage businesses to pay more attention to their internal data in the meantime. This would allow organisations to understand the pros and cons with various metrics. As long as publication was widespread, it would be relatively straightforward to put these metrics in context and understand the drivers that result in differential results. For example, broader country or industry conditions may be bigger drivers than anything that an individual business has control over.

Therefore, focusing on looking at changes – rather than absolute levels – could be a useful starting point for interpreting results. Finally, those in favour of mandatory publication of metrics would also point to the success of other regulations, such as gender pay gap legislation and how it has made gender pay a boardroom issue. The way that the gender pay gap is calculated is not perfect, nor has it eradicated the gender pay gap to date. Yet mandatory publication of this information has shone a spotlight on the issue and encouraged businesses to understand the drivers of their own gender pay gaps, and many have taken positive steps to improve equality of opportunity within their organisations.

The role of business schools

The VUCA (volatile, uncertain, complex and ambiguous) business environment is a phenomenon that is here to stay. The long-lasting effects of the pandemic, geopolitical tensions, technological change such as AI, and social changes are all combining to create added and complex pressures in the workplace (see Chapter 10). As we have shown in this chapter, if organisations want to remain both healthy and productive as the workforce and workplace change around them, line management practices will need to adapt and improve to keep up with these emerging trends. This means managers being sufficiently flexible and agile to adapt to rapid change while also having far more emotional intelligence when dealing with employees.

But for managers to be champions of wellbeing they need to be aware of their own wellbeing. Our argument is that if organisations want strong line management in the future, then a strong case needs to be made to senior management and HR practitioners now about putting greater priority on attracting, appointing, coaching and developing line managers with the appropriate skills and capabilities, and ensuring continuous development and feedback is provided to them, so they can continue to aim for best practice in the future. A line manager can either be a hero or a villain for employee wellbeing because they have influence on virtually every touch point of an employee's employment cycle. A great line manager can unlock an employee's productive capacity, but a poor line manager can stifle growth and disengage even the most motivated.

Business schools play a pivotal role in shaping the managers and leaders of tomorrow, providing foundational education for aspiring professionals and opportunities for lifelong learning. By leveraging their position, business schools can accelerate the dissemination of best practices, serve as laboratories for innovative approaches and ensure that management education remains ahead of the curve in addressing workplace challenges. In particular, they have a unique responsibility to address the growing need for leaders who prioritise employee wellbeing as a route to better performance.

Summary

Poor mental health, depression and stress are today's biggest causes of absenteeism at work, while they also reduce worker productivity. Yet, business leaders are failing to do enough to address the mental health and wellbeing of employees. The evolving workplace requires managers who are not only skilled in strategy but also attuned to the wellbeing of their teams. Business schools have a unique opportunity to prepare future leaders to meet this challenge by reshaping their curricula, inspiring ambitious visions for better workplaces and fostering the personal growth necessary for behavioural change. By doing so, they can help create a generation of leaders who understand that resilient businesses are built on the foundation of healthy, engaged employees – a true win-win. As we outline in our key recommendations below, we believe there are four key areas where business schools can make a tangible difference.

Key recommendations

- Business schools need to revisit their curricula to place greater emphasis on the social and emotional aspects of leadership. While technical skills such as finance, strategy and operations are essential, they should not overshadow the critical importance of interpersonal skills and emotional intelligence. Courses should explore the foundations of empathy, active listening and psychological safety, alongside practical tools for fostering healthy workplace cultures. Teaching should incorporate real-world examples of leaders who have successfully prioritised wellbeing without sacrificing business outcomes, demonstrating that leadership is as much about people as it is about processes.

- To create workplaces that value both wellbeing and performance, future leaders need more than technical knowledge – they need a vision for what is possible. Business schools have a unique opportunity to instil this ambition by showcasing the transformative potential of inclusive and supportive leadership. Students should be encouraged to think beyond short-term gains and focus on building resilient, high-performing organisations where people feel valued. This inspiration can be reinforced through discussions of long-term success metrics that include employee satisfaction and retention, positioning wellbeing as an essential component of sustainable business performance.
- Business schools must prepare students to act on their knowledge by fostering the personal skills and self-awareness necessary to lead change. Leadership requires vulnerability, self-reflection and a willingness to challenge one's own biases and behaviours. Business schools can support this growth by creating spaces for introspection, such as reflective exercises, coaching sessions and group discussions. These experiences allow students to explore their values, confront fears and practise the behaviours they will need to model in the workplace.
- Business schools are well positioned to drive the research agenda on leadership, wellbeing and performance. By studying what 'good' leadership looks like, they can provide evidence-based guidance on the behaviours and practices that foster employee wellbeing. They can also investigate the link between these practices and key business outcomes such as productivity, innovation, profitability

and shareholder value. This dual focus on best practices and performance drivers ensures that the insights generated are not only academically rigorous but also practically relevant.

Notes

1. Throughout this chapter we have made reference to Z. Bajorek, S. Bevan and C. L. Cooper, *How to Be the Line Manager You Never Had: Managing People, Performance, and Wellbeing in a Hybrid World*, Basingstoke: Palgrave Macmillan, 2024.
2. Health and Safety Executive, *Summary Statistics Booklet 2024*, www.hse.gov.uk/statistics/overview.htm (accessed 13 March 2025).
3. D. Stevenson and P. Farmer, *Thriving at Work: An Independent Review of Mental Health and Employers*, London: Department for Work and Pensions and Department of Health and Social Care, www.gov.uk/government/publications/thriving-at-work-a-review-of-mental-health-and-employers (accessed 13 March 2025).
4. Calculated from statistics showing total employment in August–October 2024 at 33.77 million and average sickness absence rate (working hours lost) of 2.6 per cent in 2022 (later data not available). Office for National Statistics, www.ons.gov.uk/employmentandlabourmarket/peopleinwork/labourproductivity/articles/sicknessabsenceinthelabourmarket/2022 (accessed 13 March 2025).
5. T. Allas, analysis of *Understanding Society*, wave 14 (January 2022–May 2024), using cross-sectional weights for wave 14, respondents whose labour market status was 'self-employed' or 'paid employment (ft/pt)', and all valid responses (including 'refuse to answer' and 'don't know'). Source: University of Essex, Institute for Social and Economic Research (2024) *Understanding Society: Waves 1–14, 2009–2023 and Harmonised BHPS: Waves 1–18, 1991–2009*, [data collection], 19th edition, UK Data Service, SN: 6614, http://doi.org/10.5255/UKDA-SN-6614-20
6. E. Busby (2024) 'England has highest proportion of adults "overqualified" for their jobs', *Evening Standard*, 10 December, www.standard.co.uk/business/business-news/england-has-highest-proportion-of-adults-overqualified-for-their-jobs-report-b1199082.html (accessed 19 March 2025).
7. L. Bocock, J. M. Del Pozo Segura and J. Hillary, 'The Skills Imperative 2035: Rethinking Skills Gaps and Solutions', National Foundation for Educational Research, www.nfer.ac.uk/publications/the-skills-imperative-2035-rethinking-skills-gaps-and-solutions/ (accessed 13 March 2025).
8. K. Enomoto (2024) 'Good employee mental health starts at the top', McKinsey & Company, 29 May, www.mckinsey.com/~/media/mckinsey/email/rethink/2024/05/2024-05-29f.html (accessed 13 March 2025).
9. T. Allas, analysis of *Understanding Society*, wave 14 (January 2022–May 2024), using wave 14 cross-sectional weights, respondents whose labour market status was 'self-employed' or 'paid employment (ft/pt)', and all valid responses (including 'refuse to answer' and 'don't know').

10 T. Allas, analysis of *Understanding Society*, wave 14 (January 2022–May 2024), using cross-sectional weights for wave 14, respondents whose labour market status was 'self-employed' or 'paid employment (ft/pt)', and all valid responses (including 'refuse to answer' and 'don't know'). Low work-related wellbeing was defined as anyone responding that work made them feel X 'All', 'Most', or 'Some of the time', and where X was any of tense, uneasy, worried, depressed, gloomy or miserable.

11 T. Allas, analysis of *Understanding Society*, wave 14 (January 2022–May 2024), using wave 14 cross-sectional weights, respondents whose labour market status was 'self-employed' or 'paid employment (ft/pt)', and all valid responses (including 'refuse to answer' and 'don't know'). Figures shown include those who responded 'All', 'Most' or 'Some' of the time.

12 C. S. Bellet, J-E. De Neve and G. Ward (2023) 'Does employee happiness have an impact on productivity?' *Management Science*, 70(3), https://doi.org/10.1287/mnsc.2023.4766

13 V. Minni, (2024, November) 'Making the invisible hand visible: managers and the allocation of workers to jobs', www.dropbox.com/scl/fi/886uesjzt4mjkdt2vzh2y/Minni_JMP.pdf?rlkey=glt2vftela6j84fns16yj6wqy&e=1&dl=0 (accessed 6 May 2025).

14 Meet the psychological needs of your people—all your people, McKinsey Quarterly, June 2022. https://www.mckinsey.com/capabilities/people-and-organizational-performance/our-insights/meet-the-psychological-needs-of-your-people-all-your-people (accessed 6 May 2025).

15 T. Allas and M. Mugayar-Baldocchi (2024) 'The hidden costs of quiet quitting, quantified', *The McKinsey UK Blog*, 28 February, https://www.mckinsey.com/uk/our-insights/the-mckinsey-uk-blog/the-hidden-costs-of-quiet-quitting-quantified (accessed 6 May 2025); J. De Smet, M. Mugayar-Baldocchi, A. Reich and J. Schaninger, 'Some employees are destroying value. Others are building it. Do you know the difference?' *McKinsey Quarterly*, 11 September, www.mckinsey.com/capabilities/people-and-organizational-performance/our-insights/some-employees-are-destroying-value-others-are-building-it-do-you-know-the-difference (accessed 6 May 2025).

16 T. Allas, analysis of ISSP Research Group (2017). International Social Survey Programme: Work Orientations IV – ISSP 2015. GESIS Data Archive, Cologne. ZA6770 Data file Version 2.1.0, https://doi.org/10.4232/1.12848

17 A. Benson, D. Li and K. Shue (2018) 'Do people really get promoted to their level of competence?' *Harvard Business Review*, 8 March, https://hbr.org/2018/03/research-do-people-really-get-promoted-to-their-level-of-incompetence (accessed 6 May 2025).

18 T. Allas, analysis of *Understanding Society*, wave 14 (January 2022–May 2024), using wave 14 cross-sectional weights, respondents whose labour market status was 'self-employed' or 'paid employment (ft/pt)', SOC2020 sub-major group 11, and all valid responses (including 'refuse to answer' and 'don't know'). Figure calculated for those who responded 'All', 'Most' or 'Some' of the time.

6

TACKLING ECONOMIC AND SOCIETAL CHALLENGES IN GREATER MANCHESTER: THE ROLE OF THE UNIVERSITY OF MANCHESTER AND ALLIANCE MANCHESTER BUSINESS SCHOOL

Jill Rubery and Andrew Westwood

Introduction

As Luke Georghiou sets out in the Preface to this book (see p. xv), the impetus for Manchester becoming Britain's first business school (alongside London) came from the Robbins report in 1963, which called for a dramatic expansion of higher education in the UK and of the institutions that delivered it. Robbins famously envisaged a series of new universities, and also specialist institutions, that would help to drive growth in the wider economy. The Committee he led also recommended a number of specialist technical institutions with university status.

At that point the University of Manchester Institute of Science and Technology (UMIST) already existed, as did a series of colleges of advanced technology (including in nearby Salford). But Robbins wanted more, influenced as he was by the great technological changes being seen at that time. Indeed, then Prime Minister Harold Wilson gave his famous 'white heat of technology' speech just before the Committee published its report in October 1963, and this was a time of great social as well as economic and technological upheaval. Shortly afterwards Wilson created the Department for Economic Affairs to help drive industrial policy (also to challenge the control of the Treasury), supported by the creation of the polytechnics in 1965.

The parallels between the mid-1960s and now are striking, not just because of the great technological changes that were taking place back then. Sixty years ago the economy of Manchester and the North was already changing dramatically. The era of 'cottonopolis' was coming to an end, and in 1968 the city's Cotton Exchange was to close. So continued a period of often painful structural readjustment and economic decline for Manchester and many of the towns in its hinterland.

Today Manchester remains one of the most deprived local authorities in England, ranking second in the Government's indices of multiple deprivation in 2019.[1] Nearby towns in Greater Manchester are also experiencing similar challenges. In fact, the UK (and England in particular) continues to have some of the deepest spatial inequalities and regional economic divergence among all Organisation for Economic Co-operation and Development (OECD) countries. There are huge and growing local and regional inequalities in health, education, public services and earnings/standards of living.

These differences have been increasing since the early 1990s. For instance, London leads the UK in productivity by a wide margin, driven by its high concentration of tech and high value-added businesses, a substantial share of graduates and highly skilled workers and the advantages of agglomeration economies and top-tier infrastructure.[2] Many areas across the South-East also continue to experience productivity growth surpassing the UK's overall average.

According to Philip McCann (see Chapter 3), this has given rise to a profound 'geography of discontent', and inequality between places has become one of the most important political issues throughout the country.[3] Manchester, like many of England's second-tier cities, underperforms in comparison not just to London but also to the UK averages for income per head and productivity. It also compares poorly to similar cities across OECD countries, and this is one element of the UK's poor economic growth and productivity performance both before and since the financial crisis of 2008. For many people, living standards have stagnated while insecurity at work has increased.

Opportunities

Despite these challenges, there are significant opportunities. Greater Manchester has been growing its economy at a faster rate than the UK since 2022. At the same time, it has been a crucible for English devolution, with new institutions such as the Mayor's Office and the Greater Manchester Combined Authority being created. It has also been a hotbed for ideas and responsibilities to drive further economic growth and public service reform. Meanwhile, the performance of some sectors and clusters also offers an opportunity for local and national policymakers to further revitalise the city-region, albeit from a relatively low base.

Manchester also offers real opportunities for innovation, the discovery and application of new technologies, and broader economic growth (see Chapter 2). In turn this can help catalyse wider growth throughout the region and in the country as a whole. But there are few guarantees and, even if successful in these ambitions, the city-region must also tackle long-standing poverty and inequality.

All of this begs questions about the role of the University of Manchester (UoM) and Alliance Manchester Business School (AMBS) in both understanding and helping to drive change in the local and regional economy, and their role in helping both to reduce inequalities and to create decent work and a more inclusive society, all themes which we explore in this chapter. After all, both institutions were originally founded precisely to understand and tackle societal challenges such as these, as well as to help local businesses and industries to prosper. That remains just as true today, and perhaps more than ever before.

Moving work and employment up the agenda

The promotion of an inclusive society can be achieved only if all can benefit from decent work, because it is hard for individuals and their households to thrive if they do not have access to secure and productive work that enables them to plan their lives.[4]

Businesses are the architects of the labour market and can organise work in different ways, yet business schools allocate very little time in their curriculums or research priorities for discussing the different ways in which work and employment can be, and have been, organised. Business schools do, of course, address the core decisions that affect work and employment. But these issues may hide under topics such as business strategy where the work and employment implications of investment or divestment decisions, outsourcing, technological adoption or even budget changes may remain unspoken or presented as the only option and inevitable.

The war for talent

When business schools do engage in issues related to work and employment, the focus is primarily on those in leadership or high skilled positions. This is not surprising, as these are the positions that the students – whether undergraduate, masters or MBA candidates – aspire to and which thus attract most interest. A key issue, however, is where the pool of talent for these leadership positions should come from and what can be done to expand that pool. What characterises these debates on talent (often referred to as the 'war for talent') and on the actual practices of business is the dominant assumption that the supply of real talent is very limited. It is a depressing state of affairs that in a world of mass higher education and greater global mobility we should still apparently be facing a shortage of talented individuals.

The focus when filling a vacancy tends to be on how to find ways to attract or retain exceptional individuals. These individuals are mainly identified through a selection process increasingly dominated by headhunters whose criteria include that they should already have made their mark in a similar job.[5] This approach is in itself a cause of the apparent talent shortage that has been used to justify the rise in top salaries.[6] So, we need to ask if the war for talent is in part responsible for the widening of inequality in past decades. These problems may be particularly acute in the UK, where there is a major reluctance among businesses to train and develop talent and a desire to hire only those proven to be able to deliver from day one. One risk is that business schools do not challenge this narrow focus and its implications for inequalities. As the late and distinguished AMBS scholar Mick Marchington observed in his last publication, the human resource management profession is in danger of being 'too busy looking up to see where it is going longer term'.[7] Instead of only concerning itself with talent recruitment for the C-suite, the human resources profession should be concerned to develop the talents and contributions of all an organisation's employees so as to improve both inclusion and productivity.

Who actually has the opportunity to compete in the talent contest starts far earlier in the UK education system than in higher education. Business schools, along with most of higher education, may be only too ready to limit the definition of talent to those who have already developed it through a combination of fortunate family support, organisational support and a bit of individual talent mixed in. As a country, we are not very good at giving second chances to those who have missed out on educational opportunities earlier on. If we want to make a difference to the place in which our business school is located, more opportunities for second chances have to benefit the local resident population, as those needing second chances are more likely to have put roots down in the community and to be less able to relocate. So, expanding the pool of those in contention for higher-level jobs matters. But so does improving employment conditions and opportunities for those unlikely to be able to seek high-status jobs but whose work is vital for themselves, their households and also, often, for the wider society.

Investment priorities in good jobs

The Greater Manchester Independent Inequalities Commission Report in 2021 identified three priority areas for investments in good jobs in Greater Manchester.[8] First, investment in frontier sectors, that is, those where there is most potential for innovation based around new technologies (namely health and life sciences, business services, advanced manufacturing, creative and digital, green industry and services). Second, all green sectors. And third, the foundational or 'everyday' economy, a concept that academics at AMBS have helped to develop and which describes all those basic things that we need for everyday life. This includes sectors like care and retail, which are characterised by low pay.[9]

Indeed, it is employees in sectors such as the latter, who are disproportionately female, young and from ethnic minorities, that stand to gain most from the Greater Manchester Combined Authority's Good Employment Charter. Of course that is provided that firms in these types of sectors can be persuaded to sign up to its commitments. This may be more likely if a new business model starts to take hold under the influence of the Employment Rights Bill (going through Parliament as of writing), which promises to provide the 'British public the prosperity, security and dignity that everyone in Britain needs and deserves at work'.[10] By providing rights to decent pay, guaranteed hours and employment protection – and voice in sectors such as those in the foundational economy – there could be a move towards better and fairer working conditions that in turn could start to provide a route out of the low pay, low productivity and low investment cycle in which the UK economy is stuck.

Specific challenges for business schools

The overarching challenge for business schools is how to make the case for promoting a more inclusive society as well as a more productive economy. This must involve attention to issues both of work and employment and productivity. AMBS is well placed to make this contribution, as it is the home of both the Work and Equalities Institute and The Productivity Institute. To make this case, new ways of doing things need to be demonstrated to be both sustainable and successful, though these criteria must be applied using a wider framework than profits at the level of the individual firm.

Social responsibility

AMBS, as a major School within UoM, is bound by the University's commitment to social responsibility. To meet this commitment it is essential to consider the role that business can play in addressing the pressing social issues of sustainability and equality. In turn, this requires a consideration of the purpose of business organisations and whether shareholder interests are, or should be, the only interests to be taken into account. Following the British Academy research project on the future of the corporation, the argument has been made that corporations should have a purpose and that that purpose should also involve doing no harm (whether to the environment or to more immediate stakeholders such as employees).[11] There are also wider international debates on what role business could and should play in helping to meet both United Nations Sustainable Development Goals and, particularly, the goals of providing decent work and reducing inequalities.

A more inclusive approach to the UK's low productivity problem

Higher productivity is the main route to higher and sustainable living standards for all workers. However, productivity leads to higher living standards for all only if everyone is able to contribute to, and benefit from, productivity. A particular concern must be that the actions of business should promote and not in any way diminish the productivity potential of many groups and individuals. Poor working conditions and barriers to progress in the labour market can be a major cause of people not being able to lead productive lives and finding themselves trapped in poor-quality work and poor health, unable to develop their talents and capabilities.[12] AMBS, through The Productivity Institute, is committed to developing research and teaching that could help the UK escape from its chronic low productivity problem. If the UK as whole and the Greater Manchester region in particular are to prosper, it is vital that all residents can benefit from higher productivity and that business practices do not harm their potential to live productive lives.

A key example of how the labour market may inhibit productivity is how it treats female labour. Even though there have been major investments by individuals, families and the state in women's education, the tendency of businesses to turn high-level jobs into what Nobel Laureate Claudia Goldin has called 'greedy jobs' that require excessive working hours often leaves women with childcare responsibilities with no choice but to opt for part-time work, where opportunities for progression are often limited.[13] This means that both society and the women themselves fail to realise their productivity potential, and without more chances to restart careers at older ages, these losses may be long term.

Research by the Work and Equalities Institute has found a general tendency for there to be under-utilisation of skills and talents across Europe among groups at risk of discrimination whether due to race, ethnic background, nationality, religion, sex, age, disability or sexual orientation. These groups were more likely to report over-skilling, defined as having skills for more demanding roles than required for their job, or in some cases lacking access to the training needed to fulfil their job role.[14]

Barriers to talent development

This returns us to the question of barriers to the development of talent. There is no doubt that many people in Greater Manchester and the wider UK are not able to make the best use of their potential and talents, but the ambition to raise the overall productivity of a country should include an ambition for as many as possible to live productive lives. This may require paying attention to stressful working conditions (from too-high work intensity to insecurity), providing opportunities to develop skills and progress in work, or offering opportunities to start new employment careers after life events – whether these are linked to family formation, ill-health, skills obsolescence or loss of jobs due to technological or market changes. Much is made of its flexible labour markets, but the UK has a very poor record in what can be considered the real flexibility that matters for ensuring long-term productive lives. That is, the opportunity to retrain and restart careers over the working life-course.

Closing the productivity gap

One issue of concern to local policymakers is the productivity gap between Greater Manchester and London, which in 2023 was estimated to be 35 per cent.[15] The 2023 analysis for Greater Manchester argued that the only strategy to fill the gap was to improve productivity in the expanded knowledge-intensive business services sector, which has grown from 5 per cent to 15 per cent of employment from the early 1980s to 2021. However, it is not the sectoral composition that matters so much as the low Gross Value Added per job compared to London in tradeable services. Manufacturing, the other main tradeable sector, is too small for it to provide a plausible driver of aggregate productivity growth in the region.

The other main change that is needed is said to be an inflow of 180,000 more high-skilled workers, namely graduates. Greater Manchester is found to be doing quite well at attracting and/or retaining its own graduates as compared to other cities outside London, but even so, a new inflow of population is deemed essential. There are clearly contributions that AMBS can strive to make to encourage students to consider making Manchester their base, although a key issue is whether companies in Manchester offer their recruits opportunities to progress their careers without having to move to London for promotion. Perhaps high house prices in London might eventually change mindsets about where high-level careers can be pursued.

All of this looks sensible if the aim is primarily to close the productivity gap. However, it is notable that these prescriptions do not spell out how these developments would benefit the majority of the population currently living in Greater Manchester.

We know, of course, that productivity growth is the main route to higher living standards, but it does not immediately follow that the most direct route to raising living standards for Greater Manchester residents is to raise productivity across the city region. In fact, financial rewards in most jobs taken by current Greater Manchester residents are driven primarily either by the National Minimum Wage or by pay decisions for public sector workers across the UK as a whole, and productivity gains for the area are unlikely to have much impact on their pay.

It is by raising, for example, the National Minimum Wage and public sector pay that productivity growth is shared out to those providing everyone with important services, and that does most to create a cohesive and inclusive, as well as prosperous, economy. As a key anchor institution, UoM already has a major role to play in promoting and providing decent work in the city through its role as an accredited Living Wage Employer.[16] Therefore, policies to raise living standards in Greater Manchester need to extend beyond attracting new high-level jobs filled by inflows of new high-paid and high-skilled labour.

The need to focus directly on the quality of jobs for those already in Greater Manchester has been recognised by the Greater Manchester Combined Authority in its promotion of the Greater Manchester Good Employment Charter, which broadens the perspective on what makes decent work beyond issues of minimum hourly wages, which are still fixed by Westminster. The Charter, while asking employers to pay the real Living Wage, also encourages them to adopt a better approach to security of income and employment that can enable employees to plan their lives and thus thrive and prosper. But further efforts may be required, for example in terms of building better prospects for progression in all sectors, including the everyday economy, through new training and skill initiatives.

Summary

The UK risks becoming an increasingly divided society as living standards have stagnated, in part because of low productivity growth but also because of reduced bargaining power for ensuring all are able to benefit from economic growth, although higher national minimum wages have done something to stem the rise in inequality.[17] Put simply, if business schools are to make a difference to the cohesion and prosperity of the region in which they are located, issues of work and employment need to move up the agenda, with more attention paid to the consequences of business strategies for productive lives.

Key recommendations

- AMBS has a significant role to play in Greater Manchester, both in supporting efforts to close the productivity gap through its engagement both with employers and students, and in promoting more innovative thinking about how to create a more inclusive labour market and society.
- If business schools are to contribute to improving opportunities within their local environments, they need to recognise under-developed and wasted talent in their midst. They must support second chances and second careers.
- Universities and business schools need to care much more about the city-region and regional/national growth than in recent years. In this region, that's why innovation initiatives such as Unit M (see Chapter 2) or helping to build capacity at Greater Manchester Combined Authority as it takes on new powers and responsibilities are so important.
- We can learn so many lessons about our current and future purpose from our own history. For instance, both UoM and AMBS were created to support and improve social and economic conditions in Manchester and its surrounding regions. Much of the School's practical approach, desire to challenge and to 'do things differently' comes from the wider culture, traditions and history of the city.

Notes

1 Ministry of Housing, Communities and Local Government (2019) *The English Indices of Deprivation 2019*, Table 4.8, https://assets.publishing.service.gov.uk/

media/5d8b364ced915d03709e3cf2/IoD2019_Research_Report.pdf (accessed 6 May 2025).
2. The Productivity Institute (2025) *Regional Productivity Agenda 2025: A Guide to the Productivity Performance of the English Regions and Devolved Nations*, Manchester: The Productivity Institute, www.productivity.ac.uk/research/the-regional-productivity-agenda/ (accessed 6 May 2025).
3. B. Duffy, R. Hesketh, K. Hewlett, R. Benson and A. Wager (2021) *Unequal Britain: Attitudes to Inequalities after Covid-19*, Policy Institute, King's College London, https://kclpure.kcl.ac.uk/portal/en/publications/unequal-britain-attitudes-to-inequalities-after-covid-19 (accessed 6 May 2025).
4. G. Bosch (2004) 'Towards a new standard employment relationship in Western Europe', *British Journal of Industrial Relations*, 42(4): 617–36; J. Rubery, D. Grimshaw, A. Keizer and M. Johnson (2018) 'Challenges and contradictions in the "normalising" of precarious work', *Work, Employment & Society*, 32(3): 509–27, https://doi.org/10.1177/0950017017751790
5. J. R. Faulconbridge, J. V. Beaverstock, S. Hall and A. Hewitson (2009) 'The "war for talent": the gatekeeper role of executive search firms in elite labour markets', *Geoforum*, 40(5): 800–08, https://doi.org/10.1016/j.geoforum.2009.02.001
6. P. Brown, H. Lauder and J. Sung (2015) 'Higher education, corporate talent and the stratification of knowledge work in the global labour market', in P. Brown, H. Lauder and J. Sung (eds) *World Yearbook of Education – Elites, Privilege and Excellence: The National and Global Redefinition of Educational Advantage*, Abingdon: Routledge.
7. M. Marchington (2015) 'Human resource management (HRM): too busy looking up to see where it is going longer term?' *Human Resource Management Review*, 25(2): 176–87, https://doi.org/10.1016/j.hrmr.2015.01.007
8. The Greater Manchester Independent Inequalities Commission (2021) *The Next Level: Good Lives for All in Greater Manchester*, www.greatermanchester-ca.gov.uk/media/4605/the-next-level-good-lives-for-all-in-greater-manchester.pdf (accessed 6 May 2025).
9. The Foundational Economy Collective, J. Froud, S. Johal, M. Moran, A. Salento and K. Williams (2018) *Foundational Economy: The Infrastructure of Everyday Life* (Manchester Capitalism), Manchester: Manchester University Press.
10. Government UK (2024) *Factsheet: Employment Rights Bill Overview*, https://assets.publishing.service.gov.uk/media/6752f32a14973821ce2a6cc2/employment-rights-bill-overview.pdf (accessed 6 May 2025).
11. British Academy (2021) *Policy and Practice for Purposeful Business*, London: British Academy, www.thebritishacademy.ac.uk/publications/policy-and-practice-for-purposeful-business/ (accessed 6 May 2025); C. Mayer (2021) *Prosperity: Better Business Makes the Greater Good*, Oxford: Oxford University Press.
12. J. Rubery, I. Bi-Swinglehurst and A. Rafferty (2023) *Gender and Productivity*, Working Paper No. 032, Manchester: The Productivity Institute.
13. C. Goldin (2021) *Career and Family: Women's Century-long Journey toward Equity*, Princeton: Princeton University Press.

14 A. Rafferty (2020) 'Skill underutilization and under-skilling in Europe: the role of workplace discrimination', *Work, Employment and Society*, 34(2): 317–35, https://doi.org/10.1177/0950017019865692
15 P. Brandily, M. Brewer, N. Cominetti, M. Coombes, A. Corlett, L. Judge, F. Odamtten, H. Overman, C. Pacitti, G. Rodrigues, K. Shah, P. Swinney and L. Try (2023) *A tale of two cities (Part 2): A plausible strategy for productivity growth in Greater Manchester and beyond*, Resolution Foundation, https://economy2030.resolutionfoundation.org/reports/a-tale-of-two-cities-part-2/ (accessed 13 March 2025).
16 University of Manchester (2019) 'University of Manchester officially accredited as Living Wage Employer', Press release, 14 March, www.manchester.ac.uk/about/news/living-wage-employer/ (accessed 6 May 2025).
17 S. Machin (2024) 'Real wages, inequality and living standards', Paper CEPEA066, Centre for Economic Performance, London School of Economics, https://cep.lse.ac.uk/pubs/download/ea066.pdf (accessed 6 May 2025).

7

RED PILL OR BLUE PILL? DO WE SHAPE AI'S FUTURE, OR DO WE ALLOW IT TO SHAPE US?

Michelle Carter and Richard Allmendinger

Introduction

Much like the choice in the film *The Matrix*, humanity faces a decision. Do we actively engage with artificial intelligence's (AI) challenges and shape its future (red pill), or do we passively adapt to its influence (blue pill), allowing it to drive change – and change us – without critical oversight?

The emergence of generative AI and foundation models such as OpenAI's GPT-4, Google Gemini and Meta's LLaMA has pushed AI beyond simple automation. It's no longer just a behind-the-scenes tool for business efficiency, it's actively shaping decisions in healthcare, education, governance and even creative industries. But AI isn't just transforming institutions. It's woven into our personal lives, shaping how we consume news, shop, interact on social media and even form relationships. From AI-curated news feeds and personal assistants to dating app algorithms and AI-generated content, it's influencing what we see, how we connect and the choices we make – often in ways we don't fully recognise.

Yet there is a growing tension between the speed of technological innovation and humanity's ability to adapt, govern and control that progress. In particular, there are mounting concerns that AI could replace human roles in decision making, creating an imbalance where humans lose their place in shaping outcomes. Yes, AI will undoubtedly be a powerful enabler of human potential. But it is also a force that risks diminishing human agency, particularly as it embeds itself into high-stakes domains once thought to require distinctly human judgement. How do we ensure that AI serves human interests rather than advancing unchecked? How do we stay active participants in its evolution, rather than passive recipients of its effects? How do we embrace AI's dual nature as both an enabler of human potential and a potential source of dependency? And at what point does AI's empowerment cross the line into over-reliance?

In this chapter we argue that original thinking, the very ethos of Alliance Manchester Business School (AMBS), can provide a solution to this conundrum. Rather than seeing AI as a tool that automates or replaces human effort, an original-thinking mindset will empower humans to collaborate with AI, guiding its development in ways that align with our values and needs. We begin by focusing on the opportunities and challenges around the growing use of AI in healthcare, before looking more specifically at education and how AI is reshaping our own sector and how business schools should respond. We conclude with a look at how universities are also uniquely placed to influence how AI technologies develop in their region, and at how academics can take the lead in ensuring that such technologies are developed responsibly and ethically.

Original thinking, the ability to creatively and critically reflect on technology's role in our world, allows us to continuously challenge the assumptions of what AI can and should do. If we engage creatively and intentionally with AI, we retain the power to control its trajectory, rather than letting it shape us. Original thinking ensures that AI remains a tool for empowerment, not control.

AI in healthcare: driving major innovation

In this section we look at what lessons can be learned from the fast development of AI in healthcare, and how we can ensure AI serves everyone fairly and effectively.

Today AI is continuing to drive major innovation in the healthcare sector, from faster diagnostics and personalised treatments to smarter hospital management. For instance, here in the UK AI is already revolutionising diagnostics by enabling faster and more accurate disease detection. To give but one example, at the time of this writing the National Health Service (NHS) is piloting AI-driven retinal scans to detect diabetic retinopathy, one of the leading causes of blindness, before symptoms appear.[1] This technology not only improves early detection but also reduces the workload on ophthalmologists, allowing them to focus on complex cases. Similarly, AI-powered radiology tools are being used to detect cancers and cardiovascular conditions, providing doctors with critical insights in a fraction of the time required for traditional methods.[2] AI is also helping to tailor treatments to individual patients by analysing genetic data and medical history, with the NHS exploring AI-driven platforms that recommend personalised cancer treatments, ensuring patients receive therapies best suited to their conditions.[3] Beyond treatment planning, AI is also being tested in medical devices. As of this writing the Medicines and Healthcare Products Regulatory Agency's AI Airlock pilot scheme is evaluating AI-powered devices that predict serious outcomes for Chronic Obstructive Pulmonary Disease, potentially reducing hospital admissions by enabling earlier interventions.[4]

With ongoing staff shortages and rising patient numbers, AI can also play an increasingly important role in hospital resource management. AI-powered systems can be used to predict patient admission rates and allocate beds more effectively, helping hospitals run more smoothly. And it can also automate time-consuming repetitive tasks, allowing NHS staff to focus on patient care rather than paperwork.[5]

Unintended consequences

But, while AI promises to improve healthcare access and outcomes, are there potentially unintended consequences from the increased use of AI in the sector? For example, could AI reinforce existing healthcare disparities by limiting access to advanced technologies for marginalised populations? We already live in a society where individuals must increasingly use online services to access essential services, find information and resolve issues. The worrying thing is that not everyone in society can do this or has access to these digital tools. For instance, AI chatbots are increasingly used in healthcare to streamline processes, manage appointments, track symptoms, provide health education and send medication reminders.[6] For many, these tools offer convenience and efficiency, reducing administrative burdens on healthcare providers and giving patients faster access to services. However, for the elderly these advances can seem less like progress and more like exclusion. According to Age UK, six million older people in the UK are either not online or struggle to navigate the internet safely.[7] That's around one in five people over the age of sixty-five who might find themselves on the fringes of a healthcare system that's rapidly moving away from traditional communication methods. These chatbots, while effective for many, are simply not within reach for the 2.3 million older people in the UK without internet access or the 3.3 million who don't use a smartphone. What's more, nearly a million people in this demographic don't use mobile phones at all. They're at risk of being side-lined in an age when booking a medical appointment or even getting a disability permit is just a few clicks or swipes away for the rest.

Conundrum

This example perfectly illustrates the conundrum we mentioned earlier. To reiterate, there is a widening chasm between the pace of technological change and our capacity as human beings to adapt. It's not just about older people grappling with smartphones and online services, although this is an urgent problem. The rapid obsolescence of technology skills is starting to nip at the heels of those considerably younger too. Mastering each new technological iteration seems more fleeting, and, for those struggling to keep up, essential services risk becoming less accessible, not more.

At present, AI chatbots are limited when it comes to nuanced human interactions. However, researchers are working on enhancing

AI's ability to recognise and respond to emotions, improving contextual awareness and delivering more personalised interactions. These efforts are part of ongoing advancements in artificial emotional intelligence and natural language processing, which aim to make AI chatbots more adaptive to patient needs. Future AI systems may be able to recognise emotional cues from tone of voice, facial expressions and even physiological responses, enabling more empathetic responses in healthcare settings. But these developments are still in progress and there is no clear timeline for when, or if, AI will fully achieve these capabilities. Even if chatbots do become better at detecting emotions, meaningful patient care goes beyond recognition and requires understanding, context and trust. No matter how advanced AI becomes, the question remains: how do we ensure that AI serves as a tool for better care rather than a barrier to it?

Applying original thinking

The future of AI in healthcare will not be determined by technology alone, it will be shaped by the choices we make about how it is designed, deployed and integrated. Original thinking will be essential in ensuring that AI enhances healthcare without deepening existing inequalities. Instead of rushing to implement AI for efficiency's sake, we need critical, creative thinking about how AI can genuinely improve healthcare experiences rather than just automate processes.

AI should not be developed in isolation from ethical considerations. Clear guidelines must ensure that privacy, data security and fairness are prioritised from the outset. AI chatbots must be trained on diverse datasets that reflect different accents, communication styles and emotional expressions. Without this, they risk exacerbating biases and limiting access. The most effective systems will be those that seamlessly integrate AI assistance with human oversight. AI should support clinicians, not replace them, ensuring that patients can escalate concerns to a human professional when needed. And, as AI tools become more common in healthcare, there must be education and transparency so that patients and providers understand AI's limitations and know when human intervention is necessary. These challenges are not just technical problems, they are fundamentally human questions about how we want AI to fit into healthcare. And that means the role of original thinking cannot be overstated. If AI's development is left purely to technologists and automation priorities, we risk creating systems that work well on paper but fail in practice.

Ultimately, AI's impact on healthcare will depend on the values, creativity and foresight we apply in shaping its use. Rather than assuming progress is inevitable, we need to ask: what kind of healthcare system do we want AI to support? The technology will continue to evolve. The bigger question is whether we will guide that evolution in a way that truly serves all patients.

AI in education: transforming learning and research

These themes and trends are just as prescient for the education sector. Indeed, AI's role in education is expanding so rapidly that it feels like we're only scratching the surface of understanding its full implications for teaching and learning. These questions are of course particularly pertinent for universities in terms of how we equip students, and ourselves, with enduring digital skills that will serve us not just now but well into our longer, digitally oriented futures. As AI becomes increasingly embedded in learning environments, the real question is not whether AI should play a role in education but how it can be used to enhance learning while preserving the core values of academia.

Government commitment

The UK Government's AI Opportunities Action Plan, launched in early 2025, highlights the national commitment to AI-driven education.[8] The plan introduces AI Growth Zones, increased compute capacity and a National Data Library to enhance research and AI adoption in higher education institutions. These initiatives signal a major shift towards embedding AI in the academic landscape and ensuring that universities have the resources to integrate AI effectively into teaching and research.

AI has already begun reshaping education in ways that make learning more personalised, efficient and dynamic. AI-powered platforms can adapt coursework to individual student needs, offering tailored instruction that improves comprehension and retention.[9] AI tools can synthesise vast amounts of data, identify patterns and suggest new research directions, enhancing academic inquiry. AI-driven systems can also be used to streamline grading, provide instant feedback and identify knowledge gaps, allowing students to learn at their own pace. And intelligent tutoring systems can support students outside the classroom, answering questions and guiding them through complex material. These innovations all have the potential to make education more inclusive, accessible and tailored to the needs of diverse learners. However, for all its benefits, AI also brings significant challenges that cannot be ignored.

One of the most pressing concerns is the issue of inclusion. AI-enhanced education could deepen existing inequalities if access is not equitably distributed. While AI-powered tools promise to provide personalised learning experiences, their effectiveness depends on access to reliable digital infrastructure and AI-literate educators. Without these conditions, students from underprivileged backgrounds risk being left behind, widening the digital divide rather than bridging it. At the same time, universities must consider the role of AI in shaping student engagement with learning itself. With increasing reliance on AI-generated summaries and automated analysis, there is a growing risk that students may become passive consumers of knowledge rather than active participants in the learning process. If AI begins to take over tasks that require deep engagement, questioning and synthesis, will students continue to develop the critical thinking skills that education is meant to instil?

Academic research

A similar concern arises in academic research, where AI's ability to generate content, synthesise information and suggest new directions is reshaping established practices. While these capabilities can enhance research efficiency, uncover patterns in vast datasets and accelerate discovery, they also challenge the fundamental nature of scholarly inquiry. AI-driven tools can help researchers streamline literature reviews, identify correlations and even draft sections of academic papers. But if these technologies begin to replace rather than support the intellectual labour of research – the process of formulating questions, scrutinising evidence and engaging in theoretical debate – what happens to the rigour and originality that define academic contribution?

If AI increasingly mediates the research process, automating tasks that once required interpretation, critical evaluation and methodological rigour, it raises pressing questions about the evolving role of human expertise in academia. Concerns are already emerging about the over-reliance on AI in academic writing and peer review, highlighting the need for universities to set clear expectations about how these tools should be integrated into research while preserving the integrity of scholarly work. Worryingly, the fear is that restrictions around AI may actually drive its use underground, leaving researchers to navigate its capabilities without institutional guidance or ethical oversight. That all said, some voices argue that we are actually taking a too defensive approach to AI in academic research, focusing on restricting its use (particularly in journal submissions and peer review) rather than engaging with how it could transform research over the next few years.

Teaching transformation

What is for sure is that the way we teach has got to change. The jobs that students start upon graduation are going to change. And the way we do research is going to change too, and that will have obvious impacts on teaching and curricula. The challenge, then, is not merely how AI will reshape education and research but how we choose to shape AI's role within them. What are the limits of AI's capabilities, and what human qualities will remain essential in education and research? And how will curricula evolve to include AI literacy, data science and interdisciplinary skills? These are not just questions of technological progress. They are questions of original thinking, of how universities and business schools can lead in defining AI's place in intellectual and professional life. Some universities are already taking a more proactive approach, embedding AI into interdisciplinary research and exploring its potential to drive innovation in fields like health, medicine and the social sciences, and these efforts highlight AI's capacity to open up new avenues for discovery.

But realising this potential requires more than technological adoption, it requires original thinking. Instead of focusing primarily on what AI shouldn't do, academia must take the lead in shaping what AI can and should do to enhance the core mission of universities: generating knowledge, fostering creativity and developing new ways of understanding the world. And business schools can very much be at the forefront of these debates, leading the way in terms of preparing students to navigate both the technical and ethical challenges of AI.

Universities: collaboration and impact

Worth mentioning here is also the broader collaboration we are seeing between universities and the AI ecosystems in which they are situated, and the impact this has on AI-related discoveries. In short, universities are uniquely placed to influence how AI technologies develop, and researchers can take the lead in ensuring that such technologies are developed responsibly and ethically – and that original thinking is applied.

Manchester is a particularly good example of where an innovative, strong and supportive academic environment combines with a rapidly growing tech ecosystem that hosts a large number of start-ups and scale-ups from different tech sectors (see Chapter 2). This emerging ecosystem and infrastructure has growing appeal to tech investors, boasts a sizable talent pipeline and has strong collaborations with public bodies in the city and region. For instance, the Manchester Turing Innovation Catalyst is led by the University of Manchester (UoM) and works with a consortium of business, academic and public sector organisations.[10] It aims to accelerate Greater Manchester's £5 billion digital economy by supporting existing start-ups and creating new ones, especially in the field of AI. It also helps to develop skills in the region, with a particular focus on women and under-represented groups in the industry. With no UK city having a major lead in AI commercialisation, the project aims to position Greater Manchester at the forefront and have a transformative effect on the regional economy and jobs.

Collaborations between non-academic entities and universities on AI research and development have unique aspects, compared to collaborations in other fields. Some of the key differences include the highly interdisciplinary nature of AI collaborations. AI research often requires expertise from multiple disciplines including computer science, mathematics, engineering and even social sciences – partnerships which only universities can provide. As we have mentioned, AI research also has significant ethical and societal implications, such as privacy, bias and the impact on jobs, and collaborations in AI often include a focus on these issues.

The pace of technological advancement we are seeing in AI is exceptionally fast. This requires collaborations to be highly adaptive and continuously updated with the latest developments. AI research also frequently involves experts from various disciplines fostering a broad range of expertise and perspectives, so collaborations need to be flexible, with the ability to quickly pivot and incorporate new technologies and findings, adapt to regulatory changes and use robust data governance and security measures. Here in Manchester these factors are already leading to more structured and formalised partnerships between UoM, AMBS and external partners, with clear guidelines and frameworks in place to manage the unique challenges of AI research. This has also fostered a culture of continuous learning and adaptation within these collaborations.

Summary

Original thinking is not just about discovering new knowledge, it's about challenging assumptions and reimagining how knowledge is created, shared and applied. If AI is to be a tool for progress rather than an obstacle, then universities and business schools must engage critically with it, ensuring it supports and doesn't replace intellectual inquiry. Rather than treating AI as a threat to research integrity, we should be setting the agenda, and that means establishing clear, thoughtful and forward-looking guidelines for its responsible use. This is where original thinking is most needed: shaping AI's role in academia in ways that enhance human insight rather than diminish it.

The choice is ours. We can resist change, leaving the trajectory of AI in research and education to be determined by external forces. Or we can take the lead and engage with AI openly, creatively and critically, ensuring that it remains a tool for intellectual expansion rather than a constraint on academic inquiry. If universities are to remain at the forefront of knowledge creation, they must not only adapt to AI but actively shape its role in higher education.

As we reflect on the transformative potential of AI, it's clear that technology alone is not enough to shape a positive future. The choices we make as humans, grounded in critical thinking and creativity, will determine AI's role in society. Throughout this chapter, we have explored both the opportunities and the challenges posed by AI, emphasising the need for original thinking as a guiding principle. So, we ask the question again. Do we take the red pill, engaging critically with AI's possibilities and challenges, and use original thinking to actively shape its future? Or do we take the blue pill, adapting passively to AI as it evolves, allowing it to drive change without fully questioning its broader implications?

Key recommendations

- Business schools need to teach both technical skills and creative, critical thinking. We need to ensure that future leaders not only understand AI but can challenge and innovate with it.
- Taking the red pill means schools will have to embrace the discomfort of critical reflection, confront ethical dilemmas and commit

to active oversight of AI. It means using original thinking to ensure that AI is a tool for human empowerment rather than a force of dependency.
- Business schools can make thoughtful, deliberate choices that determine how AI integrates into society. Rather than passively accepting AI's progression, they can proactively guide its development – ensuring that it remains aligned with human values such as fairness, equity and creativity. This requires ongoing engagement, creativity and a willingness to challenge assumptions about technology's role in our lives.
- An original-thinking mindset will allow schools to maintain agency in a world increasingly shaped by machines. AI's future may be uncertain, but our approach to it doesn't have to be. By embracing original thinking, we can ensure that AI serves the broader interests of humanity, rather than dictating them.

Notes

1. K. Bevington (2025) 'Future framework agreement: healthcare artificial intelligence solutions', 14 January, NHS Shared Business Services, www.sbs.nhs.uk/news/healthcare-artificial-intelligence-solutions/ (accessed 6 May 2025).
2. Philips (2022) '10 real world examples of AI in healthcare', 24 November, www.philips.com/a-w/about/news/archive/features/2022/20221124-10-real-world-examples-of-ai-in-healthcare.html (accessed 6 May 2025); Acropolium (2025) 'AI in healthcare: examples, use cases and benefits', 6 February, https://acropolium.com/blog/ai-in-healthcare-examples-use-cases-and-benefits/ (accessed 6 May 2025).
3. BMA (2024) 'Principles for AI and its application in healthcare', 1 October, www.bma.org.uk/advice-and-support/nhs-delivery-and-workforce/technology/principles-for-artificial-intelligence-ai-and-its-application-in-healthcare (accessed 6 May 2025).
4. UK Government (2024) 'MHRA trials five innovative AI technologies as part of pilot scheme to change regulatory approach', 4 December, www.gov.uk/government/news/mhra-trials-five-innovative-ai-technologies-as-part-of-pilot-scheme-to-change-regulatory-approach (accessed 6 May 2025).
5. NHS England (2025) 'The impact of artificial intelligence', https://digital-transformation.hee.nhs.uk/building-a-digital-workforce/dart-ed/horizon-scanning/ai-and-digital-healthcare-technologies/introduction/the-impact-of-ai (accessed 6 May 2025).

6 M. Laymouna, Y. Ma, D. Lessard, T. Schuster, K. Engler and B. Lebouché (2024) 'Roles, users, benefits, and limitations of chatbots in health care: rapid review', *Journal of Medical Internet Research*, 1, e56930 www.jmir.org/2024/1/e56930/ (accessed 6 May 2025).

7 Age UK (2023) 'Age UK finds many older people are struggling to access local public services in an increasingly digital world', 27 June, www.ageuk.org.uk/latest-press/articles/2023/age-uk-research-finds-many-older-people-are-struggling-to-access-local-public-services-in-an-increasingly-digital-world/?utm_source=chatgpt.com (accessed 6 May 2025).

8 M. Webb (2025) 'AI in universities and colleges: welcoming the government's new AI Opportunities Action Plan', 17 January, https://nationalcentreforai.jiscinvolve.org/wp/2025/01/17/welcoming-the-governments-new-ai-opportunities-action-plan/ (accessed 6 May 2025).

9 Advance HE (2025) 'AI Symposium 2025: Generative AI in higher education: challenges, opportunities, and risks', www.advance-he.ac.uk/programmes-events/events/artificial-intelligence-symposium-2025 (accessed 6 May 2025).

10 University of Manchester (2025) 'Turing Innovation Catalyst Manchester', 13 March, www.digitalfutures.manchester.ac.uk/what_we_do/cross-cutting-capabilities/data-science-ai/mtih/ (accessed 6 May 2025).

Plate 1 Main entrance to AMBS (AMBS/James Maddox).

Plate 2 Executive Education Centre, AMBS (AMBS/James Maddox).

Plate 3 The front plaza of AMBS (AMBS/James Maddox).

Plate 4 Early days of redevelopment of AMBS (BDP/Nick Caville).

Plate 5 Aerial shot of AMBS redevelopment looking east across the University of Manchester campus (BDP/Nick Caville).

Plate 6 The interior of AMBS during reconstruction (BDP/Nick Caville).

Plate 7 The main stairway and student area during redevelopment (BDP/Nick Caville).

Plate 8 AMBS today looking towards the Eddie Davies Library (BDP/Nick Caville).

Plate 9 The main internal concourse of AMBS (BDP/Nick Caville).

Plate 10 The dazzling frontage of AMBS (BDP/Nick Caville).

Plate 11 Library space in AMBS (BDP/Nick Caville).

Plate 12 What Manchester Means. Wall inside the entrance to AMBS Executive Education Centre (AMBS/James Maddox).

Plate 13 The main open-plan learning space of AMBS (BDP/Nick Caville).

Plate 14 AMBS staff join construction workers for the topping-out ceremony of the new building (AMBS/Bernadette Delaney).

Plate 15 Professor Fiona Devine, then Head of AMBS, plants a tree during the topping-out ceremony (AMBS/Bernadette Delaney).

Plate 16 Lord Alliance (pictured to the right of Professor Fiona Devine) and Eddie Davies (to the left) join AMBS staff to celebrate the new building (AMBS/Bernadette Delaney).

8
THE CREATIVITY CRISIS IN BUSINESS SCHOOLS: BUSINESS, IMAGINATION AND CREATIVITY

John McAuliffe and Bruce S. Tether

Introduction

Creativity, defined by the Oxford English Dictionary as the 'faculty of being creative; ability or power to create', can trace its roots back to the Latin crĕo, meaning 'to bring forth' or 'produce'. Its first documented use is in 1659, but the term became more widely known over 200 years later after it was used in 1875 by Adolphus William Ward, a prominent British historian, literary scholar, academic, and Principal of Owens College, one of the University of Manchester's precursor institutions. His use of the word, in the *History of Dramatic English Literature*, was in reference to Shakespeare's 'poetic creativity', and marked a radical change in our understanding of creativity.

But this sense of making something new and original, now central to our understanding of creativity, is actually a relatively modern concept. While it is often associated with lone 'geniuses', we can better understand it as a more complex, collaborative process. Carl R. Rogers's defining 1954 essay 'Towards a Theory of Creativity' offers:

> My definition ... of the creative process is that it is the emergence in action of a novel relational product, growing out of the uniqueness of the individual on the one hand, and the materials, events, people, or circumstances of his life on the other.[1]

For Rogers this emergent creative possibility is inherent in all of us, not just individual geniuses, and his 'definitional expansiveness', as Samuel Franklin puts it in a recent book is 'both the fatal flaw and the enabling condition of creativity research'.[2]

Creativity crisis?

At first sight, the idea that there may be a 'creativity crisis' in business schools, and perhaps in universities more generally, may seem rather odd. Surely these institutions are creative? Well, maybe not as much as you might think. Creativity and its organisational underpinnings have been studied in business schools. For instance, as others have remarked in this book (see Preface and Chapter 9), here in Manchester Tudor Rickards was among the pioneers. He established the Creativity Research Unit within the then Manchester Business School and was a co-founder of the journal *Creativity and Innovation Management*. But few business schools actually teach creativity, and those that do usually incorporate it into courses on innovation or entrepreneurship. For instance, Alliance Manchester Business School (AMBS) has a second-year elective on 'Creativity, Design and Entrepreneurship' as well as courses on innovation management and the university-wide option 'On Creativity'. But there is no compulsory 'Creativity 101'.

Suppressing creativity?

Do business schools and universities encourage or suppress and constrain creativity in both students and academic research? In his book, Robert Nelson provides a powerful explanation for the suppression of creativity in students.[3] He argues the modern university assesses everything against rubrics, including learning objectives and model answers. He observes how an intelligent, conscientious and diligent student is equipped to do well in these circumstances, as (s)he will do the readings, marshal the material and feed back to the marker the 'expected answer'.[4] The more 'expected points' that are made, the higher the mark. By contrast, the student who submits work which answers the question in an unusual, creative way receives neither recognition nor reward for this approach. The 'expected points' are not made, so the mark is low. Students wishing to achieve high grades quickly realise, if they did not already, that compliance and conformity are required, not creativity.

Nelson argues that one of the reasons for our suppressing creativity is that, in contrast to more conventional social science rubrics, it is hard to measure and assess creativity reliably: 'The more a student is creative, the more any two assessors looking at the same piece of work are likely to come to different conclusions about its merit.'[5] Rather than find ways of accommodating an important dimension of students' development, we eliminate it because it cannot be measured. It is a situation that is certainly not helped by the increasingly large classes that are commonplace in business schools, and the preponderance of lectures and seminars as the dominant modes of teaching.

Academic research

What, then, about academic research? Surely that is creative? Well, yes and no. Despite some attempts to push back and encourage greater inclusivity, we argue that research activities are subject to behavioural incentives which result in norming behaviours, just as among students. Ultimately, for both students and research staff, performance is about metrics, but the metrics are imperfect measures of what we want. Yet metrics combine with incentives, which then influence behaviours – what to do and what not to do. Put another way, business schools produce two major 'products' – graduates and research, the latter primarily in the form of publications, themselves overwhelmingly in the form of journal articles. In both cases outputs are imperfectly assessed for quality. For instance, students may get a first, 2.1, 2.2 or third, and, as we have argued above, the conscientious and diligent may well end up with a first, while the highly creative student who does not conform may well get a 2.2.

It is not dissimilar with research. Outputs, particularly journal articles, are routinely graded by the quality of the journal they appear in (see Chapter 9). But highly regarded journals do not, generally, encourage creativity. They tend instead to encourage conformity (to theories and methods), diligence and persistence. Meanwhile, the 'publish or perish' culture also encourages the overproduction of research papers at the cost of doing other things.

A balance therefore needs to be struck between academia that responds to pressing global challenges, and curiosity-driven research. Indeed, are we creating enough space for that curiosity to really thrive? In this chapter we explore whether academia is suffering from a 'creativity crisis' and, if so, what are the causes and what can be done to reverse the trend.

What is creativity?

Creativity is typically associated with artistic expression, especially by the great artists, musicians, writers and composers. Despite studies highlighting the role of institutions and supporting systems as much as individual genius, such 'big C' creativity is almost always associated with individual people, especially fabled artists.[6] The 2019 Organisation for Economic Co-operation and Development (OECD) Creative Thinking Framework defines 'Big C' creativity and 'little c' creativity, both of which may be easily imagined as part of a university's research and learning context.[7]

The former suggests that 'creative thinking be paired with significant talent and expertise in a particular area, as well as the recognition from society that the product has value'. The latter defines more everyday creativity. But the idea of the single creative genius is not what we have in mind. We are not proposing that business school students and academics should strive for that old-fashioned view which would take Picasso or van Gogh as a role model, or even see the creative arts as the default model of creativity.

Indeed, distinctions between creativity across disciplines are increasingly porous. Kim van Broekhoven and colleagues' recent research shows that 'creativity in STEM [science, technology, engineering and maths]' is similar to creativity in the arts.[8] They both rely on being open to new ideas, having confidence in creative capabilities, employ divergent thinking to generate multiple ideas or options and apply creativity to artefacts or products.

We are, in our analysis of creativity in business schools, instead concerned with 'little c' creativity, which we are all capable of. Conjuring a meal from the contents of your near-empty fridge may well require some 'little c' creativity, and related behaviours such as imagination and bricolage. Or, stepping up a level, what concerns us is 'pro-c' creativity, which is applying creativity in a professional setting, such as in a business, an entrepreneurial venture or research projects. Pro-c creativity is the type of creativity applied by leading design and engineering consultancies. It involves trying to devise new solutions rather than just accepting existing ones, and is linked to innovation agendas. Such innovation-related work can be enhancing through the use of creativity tools or techniques, but these are not obligatory. It is typically purpose- or goal-oriented, and 'curiosity-fueled', and not entirely unconstrained by end-goal and time and other resource constraints. This creativity is part of a process of thinking in original ways about situations and engaging in purposeful problem-solving matters.

Does creativity matter, and why?

There are two broad arguments as to why creativity matters. One is top-down, which is that creativity is good for the economy, society and the planet. The other is bottom-up, which is that learning to be creative, and especially creative in pursuit of purposes or goals, is life enhancing and fulfilling. Our world is changing, perhaps at a faster rate than ever, although, paradoxically, economic growth is slowing. Climate change threatens our very existence. Artificial intelligence (AI) may destroy our jobs. The optimists think that AI will create new opportunities. But, of course, the people who did the work destroyed by AI may be ill-equipped to do the new work.

It is worth pausing to contemplate what AI will do to the 'knowledge work' that our students mostly aspire to do (see Chapter 7). What will 'knowledge work' look like in 2065, when AMBS celebrates its centenary? It's a fair bet that 'knowing' will have been transformed. Already, old-style rote learning of facts and figures is largely pointless, given these can be accessed at a moment's notice. Ironically, the type of diligent, textbook answer that we reward our students for writing is exactly the sort of answer we can expect AI to excel at. But what is likely to become ever more important is knowing how to put unusually combined fragments of knowledge together into new combinations that are effective.

Creativity and innovation often involve generating elusive new combinations. Henry Ford did this when he brought together the elements for mass car production. As he said, 'I invented nothing new. I simply assembled the discoveries of other men.'[9] If we have only one 'block of knowledge', we can make only one thing. But if we have two, we can make three (A, B and AB), or four, if order matters, (A, B, AB and BA). But as the number of blocks becomes large, the number of possible combinations (or permutations) becomes enormous. As the number of blocks or silos has increased, so the potential for finding value through interconnections is increased too.

But such behaviour goes largely unrewarded in academia. Academic knowledge is predominantly produced and taught within blocks of knowledge or silos. The structure of the modern business school largely reflects the functional structure of large industrial corporations. There are departments for marketing, operations, supply-chain management, finance, strategy etc. And within business schools these are taught as separate subjects by subject experts. Our conscientious and diligent student knows when writing a marketing assignment to draw exclusively on the marketing readings and materials. Our creative student, on the other hand, might see something taught in supply-chain management as highly relevant to the challenge posed in a marketing assignment. Yet, in our currently siloed model, this insight would go unrewarded.

Holistic knowledge

We live in a post-industrial age. Most students will not spend their working lives in the marketing or supply-chain management department of a giant corporation. More systemic and holistic knowledge is needed, not least in the project-based and creative industries which are growing rapidly and which typically require creativity from people with different backgrounds and skillsets who work together in teams to achieve uncertain ends. For instance, at the University of Manchester an MA module in Publishing is co-taught by industry professionals with backgrounds in sales, marketing, rights and editorial, alongside colleagues with expertise in these areas from across the Faculty of Humanities.

Such interdisciplinary modules and alternate modes of assessment offer opportunities for business schools to learn from. And innovation in teaching and assessment is needed. A recent Harvard Business Review Analytic Services study conducted in partnership with Canva found that 96 per cent of survey respondents agreed that creative ideas are essential to an organisation's long-term success and performance, a near-universal consensus that creativity is not a 'nice to have' but a critical driver of sustainable growth.[10] Furthermore, in the past, 'creative work' and 'production' were largely separated, reflecting Jim March's binary of 'exploration' and 'exploitation'.[11] Exploitation is about doing what you know how to do, and doing it over and over again. It is efficient, but boring. Exploration involves seeking out new things, imagining alternatives and doing things differently. Ambidextrous organisations are those capable of doing both.

Traditionally, organisations separated their exploration activities (in research and development departments) from their exploitation activities (in factories). But with the need for more continuous change this separation is increasingly ineffective. Instead, exploration and exploitation are being brought together through autonomous teams applying agile practices, even at the individual ambidextrous person level. We should be preparing our students for this future, not the future of the past.

Creativity makes us human

It has been argued that our capacity to imagine is what makes us human. The sad thing is that our capacity for imagination, which is promoted in our earliest years through play in kindergarten and primary school, is increasingly suppressed as we go through the education system, including at university. In the past this suppression of imagination made sense, at least in the workplace, as performance was based on efficiency, which under Taylorism and Fordism is all about repetition. In a sense, then, to have your imagination and creativity suppressed is to have your humanity suppressed. Creativity can involve asking daft or naive questions, such as why do cars have metal skins? Although associated with play and playfulness, such creativity is not easy and requires an environment in which the asking of daft and naive questions is encouraged, not suppressed.[12] An unusual answer may be an excellent answer, even if it does not conform to expectations.

Defenders of the status quo in higher education may claim business schools are creative, particularly in our research, and our research is supposed to feed into our teaching. Well, maybe. Or maybe we are overproducing research outputs. Hudson reports that between 2011 and 2021 UK-based business school academics authored or co-authored over 60,000 papers, a substantial share of which have very little evident impact, at least as measured by citations.[13] And we are encouraged to focus our research efforts on seeking publication in highly regarded journals, many of which do not value or encourage creative research. The underlying incentives encourage this, while they discourage innovation and creativity in teaching, and do little to encourage engaging with external stakeholders, especially through hard-to-undertake interdisciplinary projects.

By way of example, for the 2021 research evaluation exercise, 108 UK universities made submissions to the 'business and management' sub-panel covering just over 7,000 research active staff. The submissions included 16,040 outputs, the vast majority (80 per cent) of which were academic journal articles (rather than books, book chapters or reports, policy related or otherwise), alongside 539 'impact cases' demonstrating how this community's research had had real world impact. Overall, 30 per cent of the outputs were assessed as being 4*, the highest category, and 'world-leading in terms of originality, significance and rigour'; 46 per cent were considered 3* 'internationally excellent'; 21 per cent were 2* 'internationally recognised'; and 2 per cent were 1* 'recognised nationally' (with 0.3 per cent unclassified).[14]

Scenario: Chris, Jo and Sam

To consider whether strong orientation towards the production of outputs is distorting behaviour in a beneficial way, consider a scenario where three people begin work within a leading business school. Chris, Jo and Sam are, in this imagining, young academics of identical age, intelligence and aptitude wanting to make their careers in academia, and particularly in a highly regarded UK business school.

- Jo focuses on research and is especially determined to get research published in 'the top journals'. (S)he considers only the highest-ranked journals to be worthwhile; to publish in a lowly ranked journal is a failure. Jo is a competent teacher, but neither enjoys teaching nor feels particularly good at it. Jo thinks that (s)he could improve, but adopts the attitude that achieving 'acceptable' scores in teaching is sufficient. Jo prefers large classes, because the workload model rewards teaching them, and sets assignments that are easy to mark (multiple-choice exams are a godsend). All this allows Jo to minimise commitment to teaching, which (s)he negotiates to be concentrated in one semester, allowing Jo to dedicate the other to research. Jo is also savvy about networking with established academics, both within and outside Jo's own university. (S)he gains access to the networks of influence, gaining high-profile co-authors, which further enhances Jo's chances of publishing in 'top journals'. In time, Jo is invited to become a member of their editorial boards and to organise sessions at prestigious conferences. Various offers come in and Jo uses these to get accelerated promotions and/or to negotiate less teaching, or the teaching that Jo prefers.

- Chris believes the first duty of an academic is to teach. After all, the students are paying Chris's salary. Chris's door is always open. (S)he doesn't believe in office hours and soon gains a reputation not only as a supportive teacher but as a shoulder to cry on. Chris is constantly developing teaching material and is generous in the provision of verbal and written feedback to students, highlighting what is good about each student's work, what could be improved and how. Chris tries to encourage creative thinking among students, and Chris's teaching scores are fantastic – (s)he regularly wins prizes for teaching. But inevitably, Chris's research suffers. It is hard to keep up with the esoteric theories and techniques that are in fashion in Chris's subfield, and eventually Chris accepts to be put on a 'teaching only' contract.
- Sam is interested in driving change in the real world. There are all sorts of problems or challenges out there that can, could and should be addressed. Some are grand challenges like climate change or global poverty. Some are local, such as the low rates of successful entrepreneurship in Manchester. Sam knows that many universities and business schools were established to support local industry and address real-world problems. In a sense, business schools were the 'exploration' departments for 'exploitation' oriented businesses without these internal capabilities. Sam feels that academia in general and business schools in particular have moved far away from these roots. Sam, like Jo and Chris, is aware of the hierarchy of journals, but finds the publication process slow and pernickety. Reviews can take an age to come back and when they do they are always critical, focusing on what is wrong with the paper, barely mentioning what is good. It is a dispiriting, creativity-sapping process, for which Sam can muster little energy. Sam would rather target journals that are less prestigious but which will provide more generous, supportive reviews and get the paper out quickly.

Which of these three characters is likely to 'make it' in a leading UK business school? Jo would, almost certainly, be ranked first, and is likely to advance rapidly through the academic ranks. Chris might get a job, and is very likely to be pressured to publish until both sides realise this is futile. Sam's profile is particularly attractive for universities which want to be make a difference in the real world. But hiring and promotion committees have become dominated by the Jo types.

Underlying all this are self-perpetuating principal/agent problems which arise when the interests of the principal (in this case the university or school, or indeed even the students, who, as Chris observes, are actually paying their salaries) and the interests of the agent (in this case the academic) do not fully align. These principal/agent problems are exacerbated because universities and business schools are not free to set their own individual incentive structures but are instead subject to (and largely acquiescing to) various rankings and beauty parades.

We cannot design new business schools or universities from scratch, but it should be clear that the school and university of the future needs the likes of Chris and Sam, probably more than it needs the likes of Jo. How brave are we going to be in recognising and rewarding Chris and Sam, and encouraging them to follow their hearts, rather than morph into Jos?

Summary

There are at least two major problems suppressing creativity in business schools, both of which relate to challenges of measurement, which feed into incentives and thence into behaviours. In teaching, creative contributions are hard to measure. While alternative approaches are possible, established marking rubrics essentially encourage compliance and reward conformity and diligence. Creativity is at best unrewarded. In research, the targeting of top journal publications is encouraged, which distorts behaviour.

Creativity is also important for all business school stakeholders. For students, creativity is both intrinsically and extrinsically valuable.

We should be encouraging a degree of risk taking rather than only encouraging conformity and diligence. Great works often defy convention. For instance, Jørn Utzon's Sydney Opera House design was rescued from the bin, having initially failed to pass the selection committee's evaluations against the brief. Why would we want business schools to breed only those who can think in conventional, 'inside the box', terms?

We should therefore recognise and encourage 'unconventional activities', particularly those that are hard to do. Universities and funding bodies are forever calling for inter- and multidisciplinary research but frequently failing to recognise how much more difficult this typically is to undertake than disciplinary research, for which a shared language, shared concepts, shared methods and recognised dissemination channels already exist.

Key recommendations

- Enhancing creativity should be at the centre of universities and business schools. Engaged, interdisciplinary teaching and research will always require 'little c' and, as a university's resources and external partnerships increasingly support it, enable 'big C' creativity. At the very least we should stop suppressing creativity just because it is hard to measure and it is easier to cower behind proxies of quality.
- Impact should be rewarded as well as recognised. At the last UK national research evaluation exercise, universities and schools were required to submit impact cases, and a top-rated impact case was worth the equivalent of four top-rated journal articles.
- We should encourage the development of alternative forms of outputs, such as films and podcasts and practical tools. The 'business model canvas', developed by Alexander Osterwalder from his PhD, represents an outstanding example of an alternative output.[15] It is a highly effective tool which aids strategic thinking and which has almost certainly been vastly more impactful than almost any paper in the field of strategy. Business school leaders need to be prepared, with colleagues, to set their own agendas.

Notes

1. C. R. Rogers (1954) 'Towards a theory of creativity', *ETC: A Review of General Semantics*, 11(4): 249–60.
2. S. Franklin (2023) *The Cult of Creativity: A Surprisingly Recent History*, Chicago: University of Chicago Press.
3. R. Nelson (2018) *Creativity Crisis: Toward a Post-Constructivist Educational Future*, Melbourne: Monash University Publishing.
4. Nelson also observed that because students are incentivised to be dependent on literature they are discouraged from engaging in imaginative academic behaviours.
5. Nelson (2018: 8).
6. 'Big C' creativity is strongly associated with the arts rather than the sciences or engineering, where things are 'discovered' or 'developed' rather than 'created', but there is certainly creativity in science and engineering.
7. OECD (2019) *PISA 2021 Creative Thinking Framework*, Paris: OECD.
8. K. Van Broekhoven, D. Cropley and P. Seegers (2020) 'Differences in creativity across art and STEM students: we are more alike than unalike', *Thinking Skills and Creativity*, 38: 100707.
9. www.goodreads.com/quotes/506617-i-invented-nothing-new-i-simply-assembled-the-discoveries-of (accessed 6 May 2025). The cut-up technique applied by William Burroughs and David Bowie to find effective prose and lyrics is similar. It is based on what exists.
10. Harvard Business Review Analytic Services (2023) *Creativity as a Catalyst for Business Growth*, Research Report sponsored by Canva, Cambridge MA: Harvard Business Review Analytic Services.
11. J. G. March (1991) 'Exploration and exploitation in organizational learning', *Organization Science*, 2(1): 71–87.
12. M. Dodgson and D. Gann (2018) *The Playful Entrepreneur: How to Adapt and Thrive in Uncertain Times*, New Haven CT: Yale University Press.
13. R. Hudson (2024) 'Responding to incentives or gaming the system? How UK business academics respond to the Academic Journal Guide', *Research Policy*, 53(9): 105082, https://doi.org/10.1016/j.respol.2024.105082.
14. R. Blackburn, S. Dibb and I. Tonks (2024) 'Business and management studies in the United Kingdom's Research Excellence Framework: implications for research quality assessment', *British Journal of Management*, 35(1): 434–48.
15. www.strategyzer.com/library/the-business-model-canvas (accessed 6 May 2025).

9

WHAT IS THE POINT OF BUSINESS SCHOOL RESEARCH? REFLECTING ON SIX DECADES OF ACHIEVEMENT AT THE UNIVERSITY OF MANCHESTER AND THE ADAPTIVE CHALLENGES AHEAD

Gerard P. Hodgkinson and Elvira Uyarra

Introduction

In the six decades since the UK's first two business schools in London and Manchester emerged from the Franks report (see Preface), the field of business and management studies has evolved into an established series of major interdisciplinary subfields. The field as a whole has amassed – and continues to amass – a rich store of concepts, theories, research methods and related tools and techniques for advancing understanding of the many interesting and varied problems and challenges confronting the world of management and organisations. Reflecting the scale of these developments, across the globe the number of business schools has risen exponentially and the UK alone has more than a hundred higher education establishments that offer undergraduate, postgraduate and/or post-experience courses in business and management studies.

Most of these establishments made returns to the most recent iteration of the UK government's periodic assessment of research, the Research Excellence Framework (REF), which took stock of the volume and quality of the nation's publicly funded research in all fields and disciplines.[1] Like a number of the UK's research-intensive universities belonging to the Russell Group, significant proportions of the business and management research undertaken at the University of Manchester (UoM) were judged to be 'world leading' and 'internationally excellent' and – like UoM's research as a whole – the work of Alliance Manchester Business School (AMBS) was judged to be particularly strong in terms of the reach and significance of its wider impact on the economy and society.[2] These results demonstrate that, in keeping with its achievements past, AMBS is delivering research of the highest scientific quality and meeting the needs of practitioners and policymakers.

However, although there is much to celebrate, business schools stand at a critical juncture. As we explore in this chapter, the wider global research ecosystem in which business schools are embedded is placing unprecedented strain on their ability to continue meeting the twin imperatives of scholarly excellence and wider impact in the world beyond academia. In its quest to become an academically respectable subject, the field of business and management studies has developed an effort–reward system that privileges theoretical scientific advancement over practical and policy relevance. This imbalance is particularly evident in areas where evidence-based insights are urgently needed – from helping organisations navigate technological disruptions, to informing policy responses, to addressing the challenges of sustainability and economic development. To rectify this imbalance, and thus achieve wider impact beyond academia, we believe that business schools must adapt by reimagining their research incentives and, in so doing, foster a culture of stakeholder engagement throughout all stages of the research process.

Six decades of achievement

From its inception, Manchester Business School (MBS), as it was known, at the (then) Victoria University of Manchester (VUM), pioneered research that engaged with policy and practice, aptly encapsulated in

AMBS's present day strapline 'Original Thinking Applied'. As Luke Georghiou remarks in his Preface to this book, much of this early work took the form of action research. That is, researchers engaged with live issues in organisations, which they attempted to solve, and, in so doing, stood back to reflect on the more general implications of their work. This approach was exemplified by the research projects undertaken by staff at the Centre for Business Research, such as the Pilkington Productivity Programme led by Tom Lupton, which had a strong practical orientation.[3]

More generally, this approach led to key developments in sociotechnical systems theory applications, pioneered by Enid Mumford, whose work generated powerful insights into the question of how to improve the uptake of new technology in the workplace, particularly in relation to the design of office work. For example, she and her colleagues found that enlisting the participation of secretaries in the choice of new information technology systems markedly improved the acceptance of change and increased job satisfaction, avoiding costly 'work arounds' on the part of end users attempting to resist technological change.[4]

Also worthy of mention is Andrew Pettigrew's long-term pioneering work examining strategy-making processes, which began at MBS, where he undertook his doctoral studies (coincidentally, under the supervision of Enid Mumford). His thesis work appeared in adapted form as the first of his many critically acclaimed books.[5]

Research units

MBS also became the home of several significant research units that exemplified its engaged scholarship ethos.[6] For instance, the R&D Research Unit was established in 1967 by Alan Pearson to investigate how best to determine, control and evaluate corporate R&D expenditure. The R&D Research Unit proved instrumental in bringing several key scholars to Manchester, including Tudor Rickards, John Langrish and Richard Whitley.[7] Rickards focused on creativity techniques in

R&D laboratories (see Chapter 8), a move that led to major contributions to the understanding of creativity and innovation, particularly through extensive industrial engagement with the R&D Research Unit's many research and educational activities. In 1991 Rickards went on to co-found the journal *Creativity and Innovation Management*.

Langrish, meanwhile, was a member of the research team that undertook what turned out to be one of the key early empirical studies of industrial innovation, *Wealth from Knowledge*.[8] He was also one of the founders of the Department of Liberal Studies in Science at the VUM, which would later give rise to the Policy Research in Engineering, Science and Technology (PREST) department and the Centre for the History of Science, Technology, and Medicine, with the former paving the way to the development of AMBS's present-day Manchester Institute of Innovation Research (MIoIR). This evolution established UoM as a leading centre for science, technology and innovation policy research.

This enduring ethos of engaged scholarship is seen today across the entire portfolio of AMBS's current interdisciplinary research institutes, which, in addition to MIoIR, comprise the Sustainable Consumption Institute (SCI), the Work and Equalities Institute (WEI) and The Productivity Institute (TPI). The latter is a major national centre of excellence that spans several UK universities, namely Cambridge, Cardiff, Glasgow, London, Queen's Belfast, Sheffield and Warwick, together with the Economic Statistics Centre of Excellence and the National Institute of Economic and Social Research. The TPI has attracted over £32 million from the Economic and Social Research Council (ESRC), the largest ever investment in the history of this major funding body. Uniting all of these present-day research enterprises is the same ethos of engaged scholarship that was the hallmark of their forerunners at the former MBS at the VUM and the Manchester School of Management at the UMIST.[9] These institutes tackle persistent societal challenges through interdisciplinary approaches, analysing complex problems and developing evidence-based solutions with tangible impacts on business practices and public policies.

Journals

AMBS and its forerunners have also made a number of noteworthy contributions to the wider scholarly research community through the development of several major academic journals, each of which reflect the School's enduring engaged scholarship, not least the *Journal of Management Studies*, founded by MBS's inaugural Head, Grigor McClelland, as well as *Creativity and Innovation Management* and *R&D Management*. Two other highly successful journals worthy of mention are the *Journal of Organizational Behavior* and the *International Journal of Management Reviews*, both of which were founded by Professor Sir Cary Cooper (see Chapter 5). During its early years, the globally acclaimed *Strategic Management Journal* was also co-edited at MBS by the late Derek F. Channon. It is important to note that the examples we are highlighting throughout this chapter in its entirety are mere illustrations, drawn from what is a much longer list of impressive achievements.

In sum, business and management research at AMBS and its constituent founding institutions has addressed, and continues to address, a wide-ranging assortment of real-world problems demanding of scholarly attention, using state-of-the art methods of data collection and analysis. Embedded in the thriving ecosystem of the wider UoM – a system that similarly embraces the Business School's engaged scholarship philosophy – AMBS is uniquely positioned to undertake high-quality interdisciplinary research that addresses the world's most pressing problems.

Threats to the current ethos

As we remarked at the outset, the wider research ecosystem in which AMBS is embedded is placing unprecedented strain on the ability of globally competitive institutions to continue delivering research that meets the twin imperatives of being both scientifically excellent (broadly conceived) while meeting, in equal measure, the needs of practitioners and policymakers.

Since the turn of the millennium a growing number of commentators and professional bodies – drawn variously from the diverse worlds of academia, practice and policy making – have become increasingly critical of the seemingly widening divide between the bulk of business and management research that is being published in the outlets most widely regarded as scientifically world leading and internationally excellent, and the bulk of business and management research that is most widely regarded as meeting the needs of non-academic end users.[10] Simply stated, there is an academic-practitioner and policy divide which has been increasing year on year.

Fuelling this problem is the fact that the majority of outlets in which business and management academics are most strongly incentivised to publish – in order to meet the basic requirements for securing longer-term employment contracts, and ultimately promotion to the rank of professor – are seeking to only publish work that advances new theoretical insights. The articles published in these outlets are largely devoid of practical application, explanation being the primary or, in the majority of cases, the sole, objective of publication.[11]

Since the mid-2000s a long list of leading figures have lamented this disturbing trend that is so evident in our field, relative to many other disciplines, of overemphasising the role and importance of theory, largely for its own sake. Unfortunately, this trend, which seems to be gathering pace, has reached the stage where even some of the field's leading research methods journals and pedagogical journals (i.e., journals devoted to the advancement of teaching-focused research) are rejecting manuscripts that respectively report methodological and pedagogical advances, in the absence of novel theory advancement.

Even more bizarrely, the research criteria of outlets such as *Business Week* and the *Financial Times*, which publish highly influential league tables of business schools, typically determine the research standing of those schools using metrics that reflect the number of publications per research-active member of staff that have appeared in the very journals that are fuelling the overproduction of management and organisation theory.[12] In large measure, however, the research standing of business schools in these institutional rankings determines the quality of staff and students that are ultimately attracted into a given institution. As such, AMBS, like all business schools looking to compete at global levels of excellence, is having to incentivise its staff to publish in these outlets. In practice, this means that many of the School's best researchers are similarly having to prioritise theoretical and methodological rigour at the expense of engaging more deeply and meaningfully with the fundamental challenges of economy and society that are surely in dire need of such engagement.[13]

Academic journal lists

The drive for business school researchers targeting journals that prioritise theoretical advancement at the expense of meaningful insights for policymakers and practitioners has gained added impetus since the mid-1990s through the rise of a growing number of academic journal lists that purportedly gauge the quality of outlets in the business and management studies field. Although originally designed to inform decisions regarding journal subscriptions, these lists are now widely regarded as one of the most important indicators of research quality.

When used for the purposes of quality assessment, research evaluators typically regard the published quality rating of a particular journal as a proxy for the quality of the articles found within it. However, before employing journal lists for this purpose, it is important to bear in mind that the evaluation of a journal's quality is far from simple and straightforward. It is also important to note that journal impact metrics typically represent an average of historical citation patterns, rather than a guarantee that a given article is of equivalent scholarly significance and/or scientific quality to the overall standing of the publication outlet in question.[14]

The initial decision to include or exclude particular journals, and the eventual quality ratings assigned to those journals included in a given list, are invariably both highly variable and hotly contested outcomes.[15] Perhaps it is not too surprising, therefore, that there is only a weak (and unstable) correlation between the journal-level rankings reported in such lists and the article-level judgements of the independent panels appointed by the UK Government to assess the originality, significance, and rigour of the published outputs of business school researchers submitted to successive research evaluation exercises by their universities.[16]

Nevertheless, many business schools across the UK and beyond are routinely adopting journal lists to inform their judgements of the quality of the articles produced by their academics, mistakenly believing that article-level metrics can be inferred from journal-level ones. Consequently, far too many of the field's best researchers are increasingly reluctant to pursue work of a type that meets the needs of policymakers and practitioners, prioritising instead the publication of articles in outlets that are highly ranked in lists such as the *Academic Journal Guide* (AJG) published by the Chartered Association of Business Schools (CABS), and the FT50 list, which typically place a premium on *theoretical* originality, significance and rigour.[17]

Addressing the threats to the current ethos

Given that the world's leading university-based research-intensive business schools are all similarly locked into the wider global ecosystem of institutional rankings which are dependent, in turn, on the success rates of their staff in publishing in the currently accepted lists of elite journals, it is clear that no one business school can address the present impasse by acting alone. Rather, the leadership teams of leading business schools must pool their efforts, with a view to driving through the system-level reforms ultimately required to enable successful adaptation to the many and varied significant challenges ahead.

Meeting this imperative requires that business schools across the globe collectively reimagine their research incentives, underpinned by wider changes that foster a culture of stakeholder engagement throughout all stages of the research process. Fortunately, several major developments are already underway that business school leaders can, and should, capitalise on in their efforts to address the problems we have outlined, and the momentum for doing so is rapidly gathering pace.

Research evaluation

First, the redesign of the UK's national research evaluation programme from its forerunner, the Research Assessment Exercise (RAE), to the modern-day Research Excellence Framework (REF) introduced the fundamental requirement for all subject areas to demonstrate the wider impact of their research. However, it is clear from the previous two rounds of the REF (REF 2014 and REF 2021) that many institutions are struggling to demonstrate that their research is both academically excellent and having major social and economic impact. Reflecting its engaged scholarship ethos, AMBS fared rather well in both previous REF exercises from an impact stance. The next exercise, which is set to occur in 2029, will further emphasise the importance of wider impact. It is imperative, therefore, that the School builds on its present momentum and capabilities in this domain, while continuing to ensure, wherever possible, that its staff strive to publish their work in the very best outlets, without trying to publish their work in journals that, although highly ranked, are a poor fit for the messages they are seeking to convey.

As we have seen, the results of successive research evaluation exercises show repeatedly that there is only a weak correlation between the evaluations of independent panel members and journal rankings in lists like the CABS AJG. Indeed, over successive exercises, panel members have been at pains to point out that they are explicitly instructed 'not to use any journal lists or metrics to judge output quality'.[18] This is not to say that journal lists like the CABS AJG are of no value. On the contrary, such lists can play an important role in guiding colleagues in making decisions where to try to place their work, aiming always for the best possible venues. However, the fact that a given piece of work has been placed successfully in a prestigious outlet does not automatically guarantee that the work in question is of the utmost quality. Similarly, outputs that are of the utmost quality sometimes appear in outlets that are not widely regarded as 'top tier' venues. It is essential, therefore, that AMBS continues to ensure each piece of work that is the subject of quality assessments is evaluated by suitably qualified subject experts, preferably by at least two independent reviewers.

Evaluating the quality of outputs

In seeking to strengthen further the quality of its outputs, it is vital that AMBS does not place undue emphasis on journal lists like the CABS AJG, in the mistaken belief that the metrics embodied within these lists can serve as adequate proxies for objectively assessing the quality of colleagues' actual outputs. Instead, the School must continue to base its quality assessments of published outputs on an assortment of indicators. Supporting this approach, the UoM, like many research-intensive universities, is a signatory of the San Francisco Declaration on Research Assessment (DORA), which expressly stipulates that institutions should refrain from evaluating the quality of individuals' published outputs based on journal-level indicators and other metrics that conflate the venue in which a given publication has appeared with the quality of its actual contents.[19]

This essential requirement, which is entirely in keeping with how the REF and all the major UK funding bodies operate, is also the bedrock of the approach to research evaluation presently in force across the entire UoM. Going forward, it is imperative that all parts of the University continue to adhere to the DORA principles. The School and University are in a strong position to play a wider leadership role across the entire sector, encouraging colleagues in institutions that are not yet signatories to DORA to learn about why this important initiative arose and to consider its implications for their own approach to research assessment.

Responsible research in business and management

A third development that AMBS can capitalise on at this critical juncture is the growing community of scholars known as the Responsible

Research in Business and Management (RRBM).[20] Founded in 2014, it has grown from an initial group of twenty-eight founders to more than one thousand endorsers, each of whom are signatories to its seven principles: service to society; valuing both basic and applied contributions; valuing plurality and multidisciplinary collaboration; sound methodology; stakeholder involvement; impact on stakeholders; and broad dissemination.

Its position paper, *A Vision of Responsible Research in Business and Management: Striving for Useful and Credible Knowledge*, outlines a compelling 'vision of a future in which business schools and scholars worldwide have successfully transformed their research toward *responsible science*, producing useful and credible knowledge that addresses problems important to business and society ... based on the belief that business can be a means for a better world if it is informed by responsible research'.[21] It is a vision entirely in keeping with the engaged scholarship ethos of AMBS and one that we, the authors of this chapter, are proud to embrace as members of this vibrant community.

Summary

Building on the achievements of its constituent forerunners, from its inception, AMBS has striven to advance knowledge befitting of its engaged scholarship ethos, encapsulated in its 'Original Thinking Applied' strapline. Presently, however, like many business schools across the globe, the School is at a crossroads. Embedded in an ecosystem that has over-incentivised the pursuit of theoretical and methodological rigour and advancement at the expense of engaging more deeply and meaningfully with economic and societal challenges urgently demanding such engagement, it must choose carefully its future research priorities. Fortunately, the School is strongly embedded in an institution that is eminently set up to embark on this exciting journey, and is already taking many of the steps we have outlined to safeguard its future as a continuing pioneer of responsible and impactful research.

Key recommendations

- The academic-practitioner and policy divide is increasing. Against the backdrop of a rapidly evolving *zeitgeist* that is both anti-science and increasingly sceptical of experts, business schools and universities alike need to create, as a matter of urgency, a new world that they do not fully understand, and take the risks of exploring it.
- To achieve wider impact beyond academia, business schools must foster a culture of stakeholder engagement throughout all stages of the research process.
- The leadership teams of leading business schools must pool their efforts with a view to driving through the system-level reforms ultimately required. Meeting this imperative demands that business schools across the globe collectively reimagine their research incentives.
- Doctoral training must be reformed to prepare the next generation of scholars to be able to undertake transdisciplinary research that addresses complex societal challenges. Enhanced training provision should equip students in the skills of stakeholder engagement and research translation, and cover methods that bridge theoretical and practical concerns.

Notes

1. Research Excellence Framework (2021) 'Research Excellence Framework 2021 results', 14 March, https://results2021.ref.ac.uk/ (accessed 6 May 2025).
2. AMBS (2022) 'AMBS strengthens its position as a leading business school for research', AMBS news article, 12 May, www.alliancembs.manchester.ac.uk/news/ambs-strengthens-its-position-as-a-leading-business-school-for-research/ (accessed 6 May 2025).
3. J. Wilson (1992) *The Manchester Experiment: A History of Manchester Business School, 1965–1990*, London: Paul Chapman Publishing.
4. E. Mumford (1983) *Designing Secretaries: The Participative Design of a Word Processing System*, Manchester: Manchester Business School.
5. A. M. Pettigrew (1973) *The Politics of Organizational Decision Making*, London: Tavistock Publications Ltd.
6. This term originated through the work of Andrew Van de Ven and colleagues. For further details, see A. H. Van de Ven (2007) *Engaged Scholarship: A Guide for Organizational and Social Research*, Oxford: Oxford University Press.

7 Wilson (1992).
8 J. Langrish, M. Gibbons, W. G. Evans and F. R. Jevons (1972) *Wealth from Knowledge: Studies of Innovation in Industry*, London: Palgrave Macmillan.
9 Van de Ven (2007).
10 See, for example: AACSB (2008) *Final Report of the AACSB International Impact of Research Task Force*, Tampa FL: AACSB. www.aacsb.edu/-/media/publications/research-reports/impact-of-research.pdf (accessed 6 May 2025); N. Anderson, P. Herriot and G. P. Hodgkinson (2001) 'The practitioner-researcher divide in industrial, work, and organizational (IWO) psychology: where are we now and where do we go from here?' *Journal of Occupational and Organizational Psychology*, 74: 391–411; D. C. Hambrick (2007) 'The field of management's devotion to theory: too much of a good thing?' *Academy of Management Journal*, 50, 1346–52; A. S. Huff (2000) '1999 Presidential address: Changes in organizational knowledge production', *Academy of Management Review*, 25: 288–93; A. G. L. Romme, M. J. Avenier, D. Denyer, G. P. Hodgkinson, K. Pandza, Starkey, K. and N. Worren (2015) 'Towards common ground and trading zones in management research and practice', *British Journal of Management*, 26: 544–59. https://DOI.org/10.1111/1467-8551.12110
11 Hambrick (2007).
12 The Financial Times has recently acknowledged the limitations of this approach and proposed a more nuanced framework based on 'rigour, resonance and relevance'. For details, see A. Jack and A. Dala (2024) 'Business school and the pursuit of rigour, resonance and relevance', *Financial Times*, www.ft.com/content/7e81e1b6-eb08-43de-ab71-ab6c50181cc3. Beyond journal rankings, the authors of this article suggest metrics that address the practical application of research (downloads by practitioners, citations in policy documents) and its societal relevance (reflected in alignment with United Nations Sustainable Development Goals).
13 W. H. Starbuck, A. Schwab and G. P. Hodgkinson (2024) '"Oh Grandmother, what big teeth you have!" Incentives to spur scientific research at business schools have been treacherous', *Scandinavian Journal of Management*, 40(3): 101355. https://doi.org/10.1016/j.scaman.2024.101355
14 Jack and Dala (2024).
15 B. Lewis (2008) 'Judging the journals', *BizEd*, November/December: 42–45; K. Peters, K. Daniels, G. P. Hodgkinson and S. A. Haslam (2014) 'Experts' judgments of management journal quality: an identity concerns model', *Journal of Management*, 40: 1785–812; D. D. Van Fleet, A. McWilliams and D. S. Siegel (2000) 'A theoretical and empirical analysis of journal rankings: the case of formal lists', *Journal of Management*, 26: 839–61.
16 See, for example: R. Blackburn, S. Dibb and I. Tonks (2024) 'Business and management studies in the United Kingdom's 2021 Research Excellence Framework: implications for research quality assessment', *British Journal of Management*, 35: 434–48; M. Pidd and J. Broadbent (2015) 'Business and management studies

in the 2014 Research Excellence Framework', *British Journal of Management*, 26: 569–81.
17 For further discussion of the unintended distorting influence of journal lists on the publication practices of business school researchers, see: R. Hudson (2024) 'Responding to incentives or gaming the system? How UK business academics respond to the Academic Journal Guide', *Research Policy*, 53: 105082; J. Mingers and H. Willmott (2013) 'Taylorizing business school research: on the "one best way" performative effects of journal ranking lists', *Human Relations*, 66: 1051–73; J. T. Walker, E. Fenton, A. Salter and R. Salandra (2019) 'What influences business academics' use of the Association of Business Schools (ABS) list? Evidence from a survey of UK academics', *British Journal of Management*, 30: 730–47.
18 R. Blackburn, S. Dibb and I. Tonks (2024). See also: J. Bessant et al. (2003) 'The state of the field in UK management research: reflections of the Research Assessment Exercise (RAE)', Panel, *British Journal of Management*, 14: 51–68; C. Cooper and D. Otley (1998) 'The 1996 Research Assessment Exercise for business and management', *British Journal of Management*, 9: 73–89; Pidd and Broadbent (2015).
19 DORA, https://sfdora.org/ (accessed 14 March 2025).
20 Responsible Research in Business and Management, www.rrbm.network/ (accessed 14 March 2025).
21 Co-founders of RRBM (2017, revised 2020). 'A vision for responsible research in business and management: striving for useful and credible knowledge', Position Paper, www.rrbm.network (accessed 14 March 2025).

10
THE GLOBAL BUSINESS SCHOOL IN A 'SLOWBALISED' WORLD

Peter J. Buckley and Axèle Giroud

Introduction

Business schools have a duty not only to understand the world but also to extend and challenge the norms and rules. But in today's world the 'business as usual' model is untenable. In a world of rising geopolitical tensions, increased economic nationalism and wider dissatisfaction with societal outcomes (including sustainability concerns), international business schools are facing challenges on many fronts, because what happens in schools is closely related to what happens in the business environment and how firms operate nationally and internationally. In this climate experimentation is difficult, as failed experiments risk institutional, personal and wider societal damage. But vision is crucial, and to have a vision business schools need a firm understanding of the huge changes affecting them.

To help explain these changes – and challenges – in this chapter we use a 'governance triangle' model that factors in changes in the international markets in which business schools operate, while also helping schools to understand changing governmental policy and regulation, and the ever-increasing demands of civil society (Figure 10.1). The triangle was inspired by the work of Abbott and Snidal

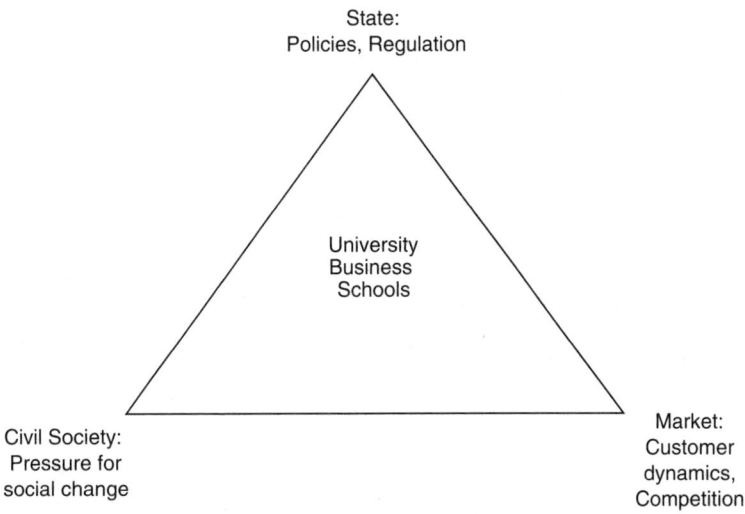

Figure 10.1 The governance triangle model – global pressures on university business schools.

on political governance and enables us to examine the roles of state, market and society – and the interaction between them – in the functioning and potential of business schools.[1] We argue that the triangle can not only help schools understand the challenges at the national level but also explain global changes that threaten international operations. It captures how the three forces of state, market and society provide the environment in which business schools operate, and how they must interact with all three both nationally and globally. Indeed, just like multinationals, they need to balance governments, markets and civil societies as they differ across the world. The interaction of these forces creates a dynamic external environment which is rapidly changing and can alter at any given moment.

The intention of this chapter is to show not only the impact of all these factors on entrepreneurship, but also the impact of business schools on the constituent parts. For instance, schools can influence regulations (through lobbying and innovation), market forces (through changes to supply-and-demand conditions of skilled personnel and teaching) and society (through seeking to sway informal norms and behaviour through research and teaching).

Shifts in the global environment

Globalisation of markets: implications for firms

The second half of the twentieth century and early twenty-first century were marked by an unprecedented trend towards globalisation, with increasing interconnection between countries and markets and a redefinition of distance linked to declining costs in conducting business across countries. It was also marked by increased ease in communication, fewer institutional barriers, liberalisation of markets with favourable trade and investment policies, ease of movements in goods and services and rising global human mobility.[2] Firms and organisations both led and benefited from these globalisation trends, and across all industries firms internationalised their activities across borders. They established foreign subsidiaries with increasing functional scopes and autonomy of decision, while headquarters gradually assumed the role of orchestrator, coordinating global activities thanks to new communications, logistics and managerial technologies.[3]

Firms initially leveraged competitive advantages gained in the home market. For instance, when internalising business activities across borders, firms carefully weighted location choice strategies, identifying locational advantages in terms of access to resources, knowledge and physical infrastructure, local competitive environment and market conditions. Their decisions to operate in specific markets were primarily driven by strategies, markets and efficiencies. In addition to internalisation strategies, firms responded to the intensification of global competition (notably from emerging countries) and the drive for efficiency by engaging in collaborative alliances and externalising activities, which led to a rise in complex global value chains (GVCs).

Today, a significant part of multinational assets is associated with managing GVCs.[4]

Global integration of production and markets has also fostered economic interdependence, linking developed and emerging countries with significant economic and development benefits (including inclusiveness) as a greater number of countries and their actors were integrated into the global economic system. Indeed, the globalisation era is associated with a rise in the number new global competitors, especially from large emerging markets such as China, Brazil, India and South Africa, but not solely these countries.

Globalisation of markets: implications for business schools

Business school strategies and activities have mirrored globalisation trends. Globalisation has fuelled the growth and expansion of business schools since the mid-1980s in various ways. At home and/or in foreign markets, the governance triangle helps us understand why and how business schools adopted a global mindset, their internationalisation patterns and the impact of globalisation on activities within their home markets. In part, the internationalisation of business education resulted from policy-based responses as governments supported the development of new business schools, while at the same time declining barriers to the movement of people boosted the internationalisation of student and staff bodies.[5] Some countries established themselves as host 'hubs' for business education, such as Singapore, Hong Kong, Malaysia, Dubai and Qatar, as the global activities of firms, integration of markets and growth across the world boosted demand for management education.[6] Societal changes paired with values in economic success, greater harmonisation in mores for elite students attending business schools and a wider acceptance of international mobility.

Business schools adopted a global mindset to match, and internationalised their operations and activities both at home and abroad.

They saw an opportunity to expand their customer base globally, especially in high-growth economies with young and dynamic populations savvy to receive a recognised education. They expanded their activities internationally, opening campuses either on their own or in partnership agreements and via cooperative strategies with foreign organisations.[7] Legitimacy became key. Certifications for business schools through independent agencies (e.g. the Association to Advance Collegiate Schools of Business, the European Quality Improvement System and the Association of MBAs), and international rankings helped schools to build international legitimacy and students to choose where to study.

Several business schools now manage operations across borders, with campuses in foreign key markets (e.g. the University of Nottingham has a business school in operation in Ningbo, China; INSEAD established its Singapore campus in 2000) and partnerships overseas. Here in Manchester, Alliance Manchester Business School (AMBS) also pioneered the transnational education model for its global MBA programme, based on blended learning opportunities in several locations around the world (see Preface p. xxvii). For all these business schools with activities in various locations, global governance and cross-border management of teaching and research activities have become key to ensuring success.

During the globalisation era, global market demands also led to an increased appetite for business programmes.[8] This resulted in the internationalisation of the curriculum, with an increasing number of undergraduate, postgraduate or executive courses and programmes related to international business matters. Many business schools like AMBS started to offer dual degrees, programmes where participants could study across various campuses and benefit from international experience. Cross-country research projects flourished, helping to increase the joint body of knowledge and challenging existing theories (e.g. the move from Western-dominated theories to new, contextually based theories). The globalisation era also facilitated the internationalisation of business school faculty. For instance, in 2023/24, about one third of academic staff in UK universities with known nationality were foreign, 15 per cent coming from the EU and 18 per cent non-EU nationals.[9]

'Slowbalisation': causes and consequences

Fast-forward to 2025 and the world is a very different place. Since the late 2000s the world economy has been characterised by rising geopolitical tensions, soaring economic, social and environmental uncertainties, increased fragmentation of markets and sustainability imperatives to address grand challenges. The role of the state has also become more prominent as governments develop new industrial policies to respond to new challenges linked to the technological revolution, GVC participation and sustainable development objectives. Cross-border tensions between superpowers are also affecting policies and national sentiments. Protectionism is on the rise and new investment policies include restrictions to address national security concerns such as around intellectual property, research and development, data protection or securing local ownership in strategies sectors.

These tensions and uncertainties have been brought into even sharper focus by the whirlwind of the current US administration and the rupture of the post-1945 world order, with all the resulting political and economic fallout. As *The Economist* put it, we are seeing the 'retreat from the idea that commerce is best governed by neutral rules'.[10] At the same time it says we are seeing the use of deal making as 'an organising principle' leading to overwhelming complexity in terms of the new global alliances that are being shaped between states.

Socio-political changes also affect the fabric of society. The pressures from climate change, increased political polarisation, the misuse of social media and soaring inequalities across and within countries have fuelled populist movements.[11] These trends have led to increased fragmentation in economic cooperation, affecting the ease and cost of cross-border transactions, leading to fears of 'slowbalisation', or even deglobalisation of certain activities.[12] All parts of the governance triangle are concerned – governments, civil societies and markets. In response to these new global realities and rising criticism towards cross-border activities (e.g. firms' failure to pay tax fairly, transfer pricing practices, irresponsible business practices, potential negative externalities of firms in host economies), firms and organisations are increasingly adopting new forms of internationalisation.

These include the rise of the 'digital multinational' that relies less on a physical presence. Instead, it demands new locational strategies (e.g. reshoring, nearshoring, divestment), novel approaches to sustainability and combining both market and non-market strategies (e.g. business-related lobbying, political connections, corporate social responsibility strategies). New strategies help firms address risks and operate in a volatile and uncertain world, yet remain competitive in an evolving global landscape. This results in the multiplication of new partnerships, collaborations and sustainability strategies with multiple stakeholders (e.g. private, public, non-governmental organisations, civil society) to achieve higher sustainability. Actors pay increased attention to their legitimacy among local and global stakeholders.[13] And this also gives rise to new types of international management strategies.[14]

Implications for business schools

All business schools must monitor both national and international trends and adjust international strategies accordingly. In a slowbalised world, markets for business schools are also changing as global competition rises. As the number of reputable business schools swells in both developed and emerging countries, these schools find themselves under pressure to offer differentiated programmes and services as part of their internationalisation strategy to remain attractive and competitive.[15] Differentiation can take the form of unique pedagogy, such as AMBS's International Manchester Method. Or it can take place through embedding research, teaching programmes, branding and impact within the local environment. In our triangle model, this is represented by the interaction between civil society and markets. For instance, EM-Lyon or Kedge Business schools in France offer tailored programmes for wine and spirit management.

Differentiation is closely related to how business schools demonstrate impact on society. For instance, the European Foundation for Management Development (EFMD) Business School Impact Survey is based on seven measures, one of which focuses on business schools' territorial influence and local impact (e.g. contribution of the school to the attraction and image of the locale in which it operates).[16] Greater differentiation can be locally embedded, and/or have global outreach. In an increasingly complex world economy, we suggest business schools must identify their differentiation advantages and integrate those within their internationalisation strategies. This will result in enhanced reputation and global competitiveness.

A slowbalised world is also characterised by new pressures on business schools, externally from governments, markets and civil society, and internally from alignment with global sustainability imperatives such as the United Nations Sustainable Development Goals (SDGs).[17] Business schools' internationalisation strategies have, to date, benefited society by educating more resilient leaders that can deal with increased volatility, and identify and respond to geopolitical and social risks. They have also contributed to capacity building in emerging markets and have exposed students to cultural diversity and promoted global citizenship. But some also critique existing internationalisation models that have environmental costs (e.g. frequent travel by staff and students), negative impacts on source countries (e.g. outflow of foreign exchange) or which perpetuate structural inequality (e.g. dominance of the Northern academic culture, pedagogies and values).[18]

In the global South, business schools have a lot of progress to make, since integration of responsible management education in curriculum development often limits itself to piecemeal additions or curriculum integration.[19] Multiple market forces drive business schools to integrate sustainability concerns within their international strategies, from the way they operate internally, to programme content and delivery method, to the types of research conducted. We believe business schools can do more, and sustainability should become an integral part of the international strategies of business schools in the future.

How business schools can navigate the new global environment

In rethinking their internationalisation strategies business schools must respond to several challenges in a slowbalised world economy. Based on our analysis presented above, we encourage business schools to rethink their internationalisation strategies in the following ways. This involves fundamentally reshaping research, teaching and how schools are organised.

Adapt internationalisation strategies to respond to global uncertainty and volatility

Business schools shape current and future managers, and produce knowledge that helps decision makers navigate rising global geopolitical and social risks. Uncertainty can affect business schools in many ways, and one example of abrupt risk was the COVID-19 pandemic. Its effect on higher education and business schools was disruptive and required an immediate response, as business schools had to rethink experiential learning pedagogies and distance learning strategies.[20] The rise of geopolitical risks also creates uncertainty that affects the way business schools operate, and their international strategies. Adapting international strategies in volatile contexts means careful and flexible planning in terms of future applications, adoption of novel pedagogies to ensure uninterrupted delivery of programmes and an ability to reach students wherever they are in the world (e.g. to overcome unexpected regulatory or climate-related impediments to travel). It also requires the development of programmes that will equip managers with relevant knowledge on how to anticipate and manage in volatile environments. Volatility also has implications in terms of schools' ability to attract and retain talent.

Adapt internationalisation strategies to respond to climate change, inequality and the push to achieve the SDGs

Some business schools already integrate sustainability imperatives within their strategies – including internationalisation strategies – but not all. In this chapter, we explained why all business schools must speed up efforts to respond to and address grand challenges, if only to address rising pressures and concerns from governments, civil society and market demands. Indeed, business school legitimacy will increasingly depend on their ability to demonstrate societal impact.[21] The Academy of International Business offers useful guidance to support faculty and student development regarding sustainability. For instance, initiatives include its Sustainability Special Interest Group, annual Sustainability Global Poster competition initiative, or partnership with UN Trade and Development to reward best research linking international business and sustainable development.

The University of Manchester is a pioneer as it embeds sustainable practices across all systems and processes, focusing on both environmental sustainability and social responsibility.[22] The *Financial Times* now integrates a criterion for environment, social and governance in its MBA rankings too. Business schools can integrate sustainability imperatives in their internationalisation strategies through strategic partnerships with multiple stakeholders in their research and teaching, through the integration of sustainability within curriculum development (e.g. sustainability-focused programmes, integrating sustainability elements within each course) and by promoting inclusiveness in faculty and student bodies (e.g. from least developed countries) or by measuring the carbon footprint of their international activities.

Adapt internationalisation strategies to respond to digital transformation

Since the mid-2000s the pace and extent of the adoption of new technologies has impacted on all firms and organisations in their delivery of products and services, and this is just as true for business schools. To be competitive in a world of rapid digital transformation, we propose that business school research and teaching must integrate new knowledge to support businesses in the societal changes that result from digital transformation. This can be positive through increased productivity from using artificial intelligence, the increased participation of small, disadvantaged suppliers in GVCs and by helping to change firms' international strategies. But it can also be negative by exacerbating the gaps that some face in accessing technologies, and through rising global inequalities.

Summary

Our governance triangle helps us to understand how business schools can navigate slowbalisation. For instance, increasing state policies and external pressures from civil societies continue to shape business school activities, including interaction between civil society and governments. In the West, populist pressures on governments to restrict migration within national borders have resulted in actions to limit access of foreign students. Here in the UK, changes in government policy towards visa requirements led to delays in issuing student visas and new restrictions on visas for dependents of students. For instance, in 2023–24 the UK saw applications from non-EU students down in three-quarters of business schools on both undergraduate and postgraduate programmes.[23] The impact of Brexit on UK universities also resulted in a decline in the share of EU staff and EU research grant access.[24] This is just one example of why business schools must adapt their internationalisation strategies to respond to global uncertainty and volatility. Strategies must also respond to climate change, the digital transformation, inequality and the push to achieve SDGs.

Key recommendations

- In a world of increased volatility and uncertainty, business schools must have extensive and acute intelligence antennae to enable them

to monitor trends. These must operate both nationally and globally, to enable the forecasting of emergent threats and opportunities.
- Critically, business schools must adapt their internationalisation strategies to respond to global uncertainty and volatility. Uncertainty and volatility are endemic in a dynamic global system. Business schools must both adapt to changes and drive them in a positive direction.
- Intelligence on markets, regulation, social trends, demography and knowledge (for both teaching and at research frontiers), must be fed directly to decision makers to enable action.
- The speed of change on many critical dimensions is increasing and developments in technology enable the increasingly rapid transmission of data, trends and events globally, such that inertia is severely punished. This suggests a radical rethinking of many decision processes in universities and business schools.

Notes

1 K. W. Abbott and D. Snidal (2009) 'Strengthening international regulation through transnational new governance: overcoming the orchestration deficit', *Vanderbilt Journal of Transnational Law*, 42(2): 501–78; K. W. Abbott and D. Snidal (2009) 'The governance triangle: regulatory standards, institutions and the shadow of the state', in W. Mattli and N. Woods (eds) *The Politics of Global Regulation*, Princeton: Princeton University Press, pp. 44–88.
2 P. J. Buckley and P. N. Ghauri (2004) 'Globalisation, economic geography and the strategy of multinational enterprises', *Journal of International Business Studies*, 35: 81–98.
3 A. Giroud and H. Mirza (2015) 'Refining of FDI motivations by integrating global value chains' considerations', *Multinational Business Review*, 23(1): 67–76.
4 P. J. Buckley and P. W. Liesch (2023) 'Externalities in global value chains: firms' solutions for regulation challenges', *Global Strategy Journal*, 13(2): 420–39.
5 B. Guillotin and V. Mangematin (2015) 'Internationalization strategies of business schools: how flat is the world?' *Thunderbird International Business Review*, 57(5): 343–57.
6 K. Alajoutsijärvi, K. Juusola and J. A. Lamberg (2014) 'Institutional logic of business bubbles: lessons from the Dubai business school mania', *Academy of Management Learning and Education*, 13(1).
7 E. Kaltenecker Retto de Queiroz (2021) 'MBA internationalization at selected elite business schools: challenges of geographic dispersion and coordination', *Journal of Teaching in International Business*, 32(3–4): 284–307.

8. M. Foster and M. Carter (2018) 'Explicit and implicit internationalisation: exploring perspectives on internationalisation in a business school with a revised internationalisation of the curriculum toolkit', *The International Journal of Management Education*, 16(2): 143–53; D. Laughton (2005) 'The development of international business as an academic discipline', *Journal of Teaching in International Business*, 16(3): 47–70.
9. HESA (2025) *Higher Education Staff Statistics: UK 2023/24*, 28 January, www.hesa.ac.uk/news/28-01-2025/sb270-higher-education-staff-statistics (accessed 14 March 2025).
10. The Economist (2025), 'Donald Trump has begun a mafia-like struggle for global power', https://www.economist.com/leaders/2025/02/27/donald-trump-has-begun-a-mafia-like-struggle-for-global-power (accessed 14 March 2025).
11. T. M. Devinney, C. A. Hartwell, J. Oetzel and P. Vaaler (2023) 'Managing, theorizing, and policymaking in an age of sociopolitical uncertainty', *Journal of International Business Policy*, 6(2): 133–40.
12. A. Giroud and I. Ivarsson (2020) 'World Investment Report 2020: international production beyond the pandemic', *Journal of International Business Policy*, 3: 465–68.
13. Z. Chen, A. Giroud, A. Rygh and X. Han (2024) 'Chinese SME's location choice and political risk: the moderating role of legitimacy', *International Business Review*, 33(3): 102199.
14. P. J. Buckley (2023) 'Corporate reactions to the fracturing of the global economy', *International Business Review*, 32(6): 102014.
15. B. Guillotin and V. Mangematin (2018) 'Authenticity-based strategizing: moving business schools beyond accreditations and rankings', *Journal of Management Development*, 37(6): 480–92.
16. EFMD Global (n.d.) 'EFMD Global home webpage', www.efmdglobal.org/accreditations-assessments/business-schools/bsis/ (accessed 14 March 2025).
17. United Nations (n.d.) 'Sustainable Development Goals', https://sdgs.un.org/goals (accessed 14 March 2025).
18. N. M. Healey (2023) 'Reinventing international higher education for a socially just, sustainable world', *Perspectives: Policy and Practice in Higher Education*, 27(4): 169–78.
19. Z. Reficco, C. A. Trujillo, M. H. Jaén, J. Volschenk and A. Amran 2023. 'Are business schools from the Global South walking their talk? Internalizing responsible management education in Africa, Asia, and Latin America', *Journal of Business Research*, 166: 113906.
20. R. Aggarwal and Y. Wu 2021. 'International business curricula: responding to COVID-19 challenges', *Journal of Teaching in International Business*, 32(3–4): 195–201.
21. O. Ryazanova, P. McNamara and T. Andreeva 2024. 'When hard-working bees do not make a productive beehive: legitimacy, tensions in societal impact governance and how to navigate them', *Academy of Management Learning and Education*, 23: 460–81.

22 In 2025, the University of Manchester was ranked in the top ten globally in the QS World University Sustainability Ranking, www.manchester.ac.uk/about/news/manchester-retains-top-10-global-position-in-qs-world-university-sustainability-rankings/#:~:text=The%20University%20of%20Manchester%20has,%2C%20and%20Governance%20(ESG) (accessed 14 March 2025).
23 CABS (2024) *Analysis of International Students Enrolments Report*, https://charteredabs.org/policy/research/analysis-of-international-student-enrolments-in-january-2024 (accessed 4 February 2025).
24 Times Higher Education (2025) 'How bad has Brexit been for UK universities?' 31 January, www.timeshighereducation.com/depth/how-bad-has-brexit-been-uk-universities (accessed 4 February 2025).

CONCLUSION: A BUSINESS SCHOOL FOR THE TWENTY-FIRST CENTURY

Fiona Devine and Nazir Afzal

Introduction

Anniversaries, whether personal or professional, are often a time of reflection. They allow us to appreciate, sometimes quietly and deeply, away from the 'hustle and bustle' of everyday life, the past and what has been achieved. In addition, they are a great opportunity to look forward and imagine what the future will be, what we want and need it to be and how we might achieve our ambitions both individually and collectively. Thinking ahead can fill us with excitement and renewed energy about new goals we want to accomplish and how we are going to do so. In the sixtieth anniversary year for Alliance Manchester Business School (AMBS), this collection of thought-provoking chapters looks ahead to consider the role of the business school in understanding global challenges and, very importantly, how we might provide solutions to overcome them for the greater good through our socially responsible research and teaching.

The chapters in this book, by eminent academics and business leaders, have been written in such a way as to reach out to a wide audience of readers including business leaders, policymakers, AMBS alumni and prospective home and international students. This final chapter pulls together some of the common themes that have emerged from this collection. Against the background of change and turbulence, the importance of research and teaching focused on the big challenges of our times is clearly noted. In the pursuit of sustainable and inclusive economic growth, supporting innovation and entrepreneurship will be pivotal. So too will be a sense of place and the need to contribute to local ecosystems across cities and regions. Interdisciplinarity will be required to ensure a holistic approach to developing solutions to problems. Finally, we will need to create and sustain leaders who can inspire trust in these changing times.

Change and turbulence

One of the clear themes emerging from this collection is the period of change and turbulence in which we live. The opening decades of the twenty-first century have been marked by seismic events. The COVID-19 global pandemic, between 2020 and 2023, led to approximately 310,000 deaths in the UK and over seven million deaths worldwide.[1] The pandemic upended everyday lives as national lockdowns limited social interaction in ways never experienced in people's lifetimes. Schools, colleges and universities had to move swiftly on delivering learning online and, more widely, large swathes of the working population had to work remotely at home. The effects on our routine practices, including on our mental health, pressures on the healthcare system and the effects on businesses are still being played out. The pandemic highlighted profound underlying challenges in the world which need tackling, including in the world of business and management.

An earlier shock to the global economy came in the form of the great financial crisis of 2007–08. Originating in the US with a crisis in subprime mortgage lending and the collapse of the housing market, it spread to the failure of major banks, a global credit crunch and governments and central banks worldwide intervening with bailouts and stimulus packages to stabilise economies. Global economic growth has yet to recover, and living standards have not increased as a result. The lack of economic growth is also closely associated with low levels of productivity. The Productivity Institute (TPI), a collaboration between ten partners with its headquarters at AMBS, is an interdisciplinary entity and is playing an important role in looking at the drivers of productivity and, for example, at how leaders can address issues of mental health in the workforce and thereby improve productivity, as Cooper and Allas outlined in Chapter 5.

Profound socio-cultural changes are in evidence too. The movement of people across geographical areas and national borders has long characterised human history. As Hein de Haas argues, migration has a 'central role in economic development and social transformation'.[2] Migration has meant that the UK is a hugely diverse country in terms of ethnicity, religion, language and culture. Manchester is very diverse too. These demographic changes mean that businesses and organisations have increasingly diverse workforces, and issues of equality, diversity and inclusion are hugely important for business leaders. Research on changing patterns and trends in work and employment, of both high-skilled and low-skilled workers, remains highly relevant to any business school agenda, as Rubery and Westwood argued in Chapter 6. The Work and Equalities Institute at AMBS is a good example of shaping good policy and practice.

International business is in an immense state of flux too, with implications for business schools. Growing geopolitical tensions, increased economic nationalism and wider societal grievances about inequalities are creating a 'dynamic external environment' as Buckley and Giroud observed in Chapter 10. Globalisation is slowing down and, arguably, going into reverse. The international environment is characterised by uncertainty, fragmentation, tensions and protectionism, most notably since Brexit in January 2020 and the election of Donald Trump in the US in November 2024. Markets, governments and civil society are all affected by these trends. Businesses will adapt their location strategies, enhance their digital presence and change their wider management strategies. Business schools will do so too and seek to differentiate themselves. Alongside research, it will be imperative to educate resilient leaders in this era of volatility and risk.

The greatest societal challenge of them all is climate change and navigating the transition to a net zero world, as Geels and Sadan noted in Chapter 1. Production and consumption will need to be radically altered, as well as individual attitudes and behaviours, and collective policies and practices. But change brings opportunities, and many businesses have transition plans now. What is heartening is that the pace of change is accelerating and considerable progress is being made. Innovation is a driving force with the adoption of new technologies and the creation of new markets, and metrics have been developed to chart progress. Yes, there will be new hurdles and setbacks. Yet the story is still positive. For business schools there is a huge interdisciplinary research agenda, especially on the role of innovation and finance in the transition period. Students will need to learn all about those transition processes and how they are being navigated.

Innovation and entrepreneurship

If one of the global challenges of our times is to achieve economic growth which is both inclusive and sustainable, a focus on innovation and entrepreneurship surely follows as Lou Cordwell outlined in Chapter 2, writing about the exciting plans for Unit M and the Sister initiative in Manchester city centre. It is not hard to imagine that AMBS will be vital part of the University of Manchester's (UoM) contribution to a welcoming innovation system locally, nationally and internationally in the future. As Luke Georghiou outlined in his Preface, AMBS has a long history of research in innovation and entrepreneurship via the Manchester Institute of Innovation Research (MIoIR) and its predecessors. The study of the environment in which innovation and entrepreneurship thrives, how government policy facilitates the conditions for business growth and the role of universities in sharing or co-producing new knowledge with all types of businesses will continue to be very important areas of research.

Students and teaching are very much part of this agenda. The Masood Entrepreneurship Centre has long supported undergraduate and masters students, including MBA students, and postgraduate researchers who have aspired to start up their own businesses and create spin-outs from research. The shorthand reference to businesses also includes social enterprises which students, and indeed staff, often build up. Including entrepreneurship and innovation as part of the curriculum is important, as is expanding the reach of current business schools' courses to all students across universities. It is not just for scientists and engineers, after all. Extracurricular support is pivotal to help students develop their novel ideas for new products or services, develop business cases, secure initial funding and so forth. Drawing on the wider wraparound services to help small businesses to scale up over time is critical too.

The Executive Education portfolio in AMBS has facilitated partnerships with large and small businesses across the private and public sector over many years. Again, it is not hard to imagine that such partnerships will need to grow in number and value, and our learning offerings will help businesses grow, adopt new technologies, facilitate new leadership capabilities and much more. Previously, the AMBS Executive Education's brand and reputation was built on the closed programme, developed in a bespoke way for individual businesses. Many of the relationships with big organisations will continue, of course. But there has been a pivot towards open programmes for individual employees and the delivery of short courses which are flexible, in the knowledge that life-long learners are busy people balancing the demands of work and family.

Many of these relationships and partnerships have been forged in the city of Manchester, the ten combined authorities of Greater Manchester and the wider North-West region as you would expect. AMBS, in other words, has played an important role in the city's innovation ecosystem, which is part of UoM's commitment to civic engagement. It will continue to do so. After all, success comes from the right mix of competition and collaboration. Collaboration is the name of the game for the wider benefit of all. A great example is the collaboration of the business schools across the ten local authorities of Greater Manchester who jointly offer Open SME, a free 24/7 programme to help small and medium enterprises to grow, in collaboration with the Business Growth Hub funded by Greater Manchester Combined Authority (GMCA).[3] Such partnerships are critical for the success of the city region.

In sum, it is easy to imagine that AMBS will build on its strengths as a significant player in the inclusive ecosystem in the Manchester city region. As an outward-facing business school which has long had a revolving door between academia and business, it has the real potential to extend the relationships and partnerships that it has built up to date. Academic and professional staff have a collaborative mindset, happy to work with other universities, further education colleges, hospitals and local government in the public sector, and businesses of all shapes and sizes across different sectors in the private sector. A business school has a pivotal role to play in sharing networks, providing spaces for working together, as well as bringing people together at events of all different kinds and attracting and retaining key talent. All these activities will facilitate the environment for innovation and entrepreneurship.

Place and governance

For anyone working and/or living in Manchester, its considerable strengths will be well known. It is a city of sport with two huge football teams. They are big businesses which have amazing global reputations and attract large numbers of fans to watch thrilling games. It is a city of culture with music at this core, also widely known around the world. Venues attract big stars who pull in the crowds. There is an incredible vibrancy to the city which fuels confidence. Politically, it has long been a place of collaboration, with local government leaders keen to attract businesses into the city. As the late Sir Howard Bernstein, chief executive of Manchester City Council between 1998 and 2017, often said, businesses bring jobs and jobs facilitate health and wellbeing. However, economic growth, including productivity, is not where it should be and unequal health outcomes are still concerning.

Given that the UK is a small country, geographically speaking, it is incredible that regional productivity inequalities are nearly the highest in the industrialised world, as Leahy and McCann noted in Chapter 3. We live in a country where the levels of productivity in London overshadow those in the regions and cities like Manchester, Birmingham and Glasgow. Capital cities have a big presence in any country, but the imbalance in the UK is extreme. Although there are regional differences in the workforce and in levels of education and skills, they do not explain the disparities that spread outside London across the whole of the country. As you would expect, the business community and civic leaders in the city of Manchester and Greater Manchester work together and also with the wider region, including Liverpool as the other key big city in the North-West. Leaders are highly attuned and concerned about the economic and social implications for their citizens.

This divide has grown since the mid-1970s as London and the regions have increasingly diverged. From the 1980s onwards, London and the South-East region, largely serving the capital, became a powerhouse of economic activity in the UK. At the same time, however, other regions in the UK were experiencing the ongoing challenges of deindustrialisation as businesses and jobs moved elsewhere or closed and disappeared altogether. While public and private investment facilitated growth and increased productivity in London, the lack of investment meant the regions fell behind and a new 'economic geography' emerged. Corporate headquarters are rarely to be found outside the South and venture capital is largely absent. All of these shocks and trends have had long-term scarring effects, made worse by the absence of policymaking attuned to the needs of a particular place and its uniqueness.

The Brexit vote in 2016 was a wake-up call to government that economic policy had to be attuned to the regions and cities outside London, and the vote added momentum to critical thinking about overcentralised governance in the UK. For instance, in 2014 leaders across the ten Greater Manchester local authorities signed a deal with the Government to devolve a wide range of powers, budgets and responsibilities to the GMCA and to an elected Greater Manchester Mayor. The introduction of local budgeting and place-based decision making has facilitated economic opportunities as local politicians have made investment decisions and sought to reform local services. Public investment is encouraging private investment. A journey has been started and progress is evident, although there is a long way to go to secure inclusive prosperity and wellbeing for all citizens and communities in the city and other cities in the region.

Like UoM, AMBS is very much part of the vibrant ecosystem of a wide array of organisations, public and private, committed to economic and social wellbeing. The challenge for the Business School is to be even more open than it is, to be even more of a great connector than it is. Sharing its facilities and welcoming all to its events should continue. It needs to enhance the impact of its research and to do so at pace, and to facilitate more spin-outs and start-up businesses among staff and students. It must support all sorts of flexible learning as a full-service business school ranging from students on undergraduate degrees to leaders and managers undertaking short courses. In Chapter 3 Leahy and McCann argued that cities like Manchester and Liverpool need to be bigger than they are today and to enjoy the advantages of scale more than they do today. The Business School has such a key role to play in this incredible agenda.

Interdisciplinarity

This collection has highlighted the huge importance of interdisciplinarity – collaborating with theories and methods across disciplines – in research and teaching. Business schools are inherently interdisciplinary in nature. Academic colleagues are drawn from a wide variety of disciplines including accounting and finance, business and management, other social sciences like economics, politics and sociology, as well as engineering, the natural sciences and medicine and health. It is not unusual for a business school like AMBS to be organised by divisions or departments which do not align with strict definitions of a discipline or subject area. People and structures, in other words, facilitate cross-disciplinary work. Teams of colleagues working together on a research topic, or sharing the teaching of a course, is not uncommon. Indeed, their interdisciplinary nature ensures that business schools are a great connector within universities.

There is plenty of evidence of the value of interdisciplinarity in terms of collaboration, innovation and advances in finding solutions to business and management challenges. Within AMBS, for example, scholars of international business work with experts in innovation. Academics in accounting and finance work with scholars in information technology as can be found in the Centre for Financial Technology (FinTech) Studies at AMBS. Within the Faculty of Humanities, the Sustainable Consumption Institute, for example, is a joint institute across AMBS and the School of Social Sciences and is the home of scholars working on sustainability, production and consumption. It examines a range of actors from individual consumers to firms, government and other organisations, and inquiry spans from system transitions to everyday practices. Sustainability, of course, is one of the most pressing challenges of our times worthy of such a holistic approach.

Other examples of social sciences collaboration between business and management scholars and, for example, social statisticians and criminologists, can be found in the Centre for Digital Trust and Society at UoM. Digital systems, including artificial intelligence (AI), are not simply technical issues and the domain of computer scientists. Major technical transformations have a human dimension with consequences for individuals, workplaces and societies at large. New challenges around organisational security, data, privacy and trust – and many more topics besides – require new interdisciplinary collaborations. Similarly, AMBS colleagues have long worked with scholars in the Global Development Institute in the School of Environment, Education and Development on international business and global value changes, including those associated with the Work and Equalities Institute in AMBS.

It is relatively easy for business and management scholars to work with social scientists, of course. They are related, cognate disciplines after all. There are examples, however, of collaborations between Business School colleagues and scholars in arts and humanities on digital transformations in the cultural industries via Creative Manchester and, in the recent past, research on the geography of the creative industries and the effectiveness of design protocols under the auspices of the Creative Industries Policy and Evidence Centre. Beyond humanities, there have long been collaborations between Business School scholars in science and engineering, notably in Maths and Computer Science. It is in this space that the commercialisation of research has the most potential, such as the work of colleagues who have developed a tool (FuSeBMC-AI tool) which improves computer source code security, which can reduce cyber security threats.[4]

Finally, interdisciplinary research at the interface of medicine and health and business and management is growing exponentially. Innovations in healthcare products and services are much needed. AMBS scholars, for example, are currently working on AI decision support for mental health services which integrates AI with community mental health services to enhance clinical decision making and improve patient outcomes. Colleagues from MIoIR are looking at the adoption of pharmacogenetics/genomics in the National Health Service for cardiovascular diseases.[5] AMBS colleagues are also involved in Healthier Futures, an interdisciplinary research platform at UoM supporting work to enhance health equity.[6] All this work is supported by a longstanding, university-wide commitment to interdisciplinarity. For instance, Professor Colette Fagan, UoM's Vice-President for Research, was part of a British Academy working group in a major study into interdisciplinarity.[7]

Building trust

Finally, it is worth reiterating here in the wider context of this book's themes, that we are all reliant on trust as a crucial ingredient that sustains business, democracy and public institutions. It is impossible to deliver justice without public trust. Trust is that vital, mercurial quality that allows you to get things done. Without trust, relationships and operations falter. You cannot get credit, you cannot create loyalty and you lose customers. It is equally important for good government and public institutions. It is what fuels democracy, guarantees freedoms and empowers citizens to bring about change. So, while

AMBS faces a host of modern challenges in its sixtieth year, the importance of trust stands out too. It is a constant since the beginning.

Our educational institutions have always required public trust in order to function. They need it more than ever nowadays to defend their role as truth-seeking institutions that foster critical thinking and develop a democratic culture. In an age of fake news, algorithm-driven echo chambers and disinformation, their role in fostering civic engagement and upholding free expression is vital. The rise of populism is seeing increased distrust, division and public anxiety. As public trust collapses, sound policymaking, human rights and democracy are the first casualties. Higher education institutions are therefore among the last lines of defence against disinformation. Their role is to uphold democracy and strengthen civic values. These are global concerns. This need for public trust transcends national boundaries, as universities and business schools worldwide play a critical role in defending democracy and combating disinformation.

Universities foster trust and truth in many ways. They encourage students to recognise diverse viewpoints and perspectives, explore differences, rigorously examine evidence and commit to critical inquiry. But this is just one part of the equation. Another part is the vital art of disagreeing well. Ours is an age of instant gratification where technology has reduced our thought spans and limited our ability to engage meaningfully with information. Consequently, many are sliding into echo chambers where they listen only to what they want to hear and are unable to conduct civil debate and understand difference. It was Gandhi who said 'honest disagreement is often a sign of progress', and without this, regression is guaranteed.[8] Equipping a new generation with the skills to keep an open mind, to listen and to test evidence is the first step to reversing this. It is critical to sustaining democracy and to understanding how to solve intractable problems.

Universities and their business schools need to ask themselves who are the people in the community that we are not currently engaging with, and why they might feel excluded or unheard. How can we build trust and establish genuine relationships with community members, particularly those who may be sceptical or disengaged?

What steps can we take to ensure that the community's needs and perspectives are actively shaping the programmes or policies we create? We build trust through active listening, by being transparent, by engaging in co-creation, through inclusive representation and having ongoing feedback loops. We do so by using data to inform decisions, by developing empathy-driven policy and committing to continuous education.

These are critical life skills that students learn throughout their educational journey. They are key skills for good management and leadership in the sphere of business and for democracy in which businesses thrive. Democracy is hard, messy and far from perfect. It's a constant struggle to sustain and has evolved over a thousand years through the Magna Carta and development of Parliament. It requires trusted public institutions to succeed and has delivered the rule of law, peace and freedom. It is a relentless and necessary pursuit.

Summary

In this era of great economic, social and political change, no business school can be complacent about its responsibilities. AMBS has never been self-satisfied. As a socially responsible Business School there is a genuine commitment to research directed towards finding solutions to the big challenges, both global and local, of our times. This will often be interdisciplinary in nature, to secure a holistic view of the challenges in hand, and will involve relationships and partnerships with business and many other organisations. It is not hard to imagine the co-production of knowledge will become more prevalent in the future. Similarly, knowledge will be shared through innovation and entrepreneurship with spin-outs which may be commercial, or maybe not. There is nothing wrong in our research being useful in a whole variety of ways to a wide range of individuals and communities in business and civil society.

It will be incumbent on AMBS to play a pivotal role in educating the next generation of socially responsible leaders while also supporting the life-long learning of those who occupy leadership roles around the globe. As Ivison and McPhail noted in their Introduction, our students are powerful agents for change, often critical of the way the economy and society is organised now, and desire better ways of working and living. It will be for our teachers, again in partnership with students, to equip learners with the important skills to navigate the turbulent world in changing times and make a positive contribution to it. Being constructive rather than cynical, understanding the importance of relationships and working in partnership with others, navigating different and diverse opinions, especially in the social media age, will be key skills to cultivate. It will be for all of us to make a positive contribution and to be confident in rising to these challenges.

Notes

1 Office for National Statistics (2022) 'Total COVID-19 deaths in the UK', October, www.ons.gov.uk/aboutus/transparencyandgovernance/freedomofinformationfoi/totalcovid19deathsintheuk (accessed 6 May 2025).
2 H. de Hass (2023) *How Migration Really Works: 22 Things You Need to Know about the Most Divisive Issue in Politics*, London: Penguin Books, p. 328.
3 GMCA (2022) 'Greater Manchester launches new leadership and management resource to help small businesses thrive', May, https://greatermanchester-ca.gov.uk/news/greater-manchester-launches-new-leadership-and-management-resource-to-help-small-businesses-thrive (accessed 6 May 2025).
4 AMBS (2024) 'Software spin-out wins funding from Innovation Factory', February, www.alliancembs.manchester.ac.uk/news/software-spin-out-wins-funding-from-innovation-factory/ (accessed 6 May 2025).
5 AMBS (2022) 'MIOIR begins major study into personalised cardiovascular treatments', 1 November, www.alliancembs.manchester.ac.uk/news/mioir-begins-major-study-into-personalised-cardiovascular-treatments/ (accessed 6 May 2025).
6 UoM (n.d.) 'Addressing health inequalities at Manchester', www.healthierfutures.manchester.ac.uk/ (accessed 6 May 2025).
7 British Academy (2016) 'British Academy launches interdisciplinary report', 12 July, www.thebritishacademy.ac.uk/news/british-academy-launches-interdisciplinarity-report/ (accessed 6 May 2025).
8 www.goodreads.com/quotes/809925-honest-disagreement-is-often-a-good-sign-of-progress (accessed 6 May 2025).

INDEX

Note: **page numbers in bold denote an illustration.**

1960s xvi–xx, xxiv–xxv, xxviii–xix, 61, 93–94, 134
1970s xix–xx, xxiv, xxviii, 42, 43, 45, 52, 61, 166
1980s xvii, xx, xxi, xxiv, 41–46, 50, 61, 101, 149, 166
1990s xvii, xix, xxii, xxiv, xxix, 3, 16, 31, 45, 61, 70, 94, 135, 138, 165
2000s xvi, xx, xxiii, xxvi, xxvii, xxix–xxx, 16, 19, 46, 68, 70, 80, 137, 150, 151, 155
2008 global financial crisis 43, 47, 49, 66, 95, 161

academic journals *see* publication
Action Learning xvi, xix
Alliance, Lord xxvii, **plate 16**
Alliance Manchester Business School (AMBS) 107
    Centre for Financial Technology Studies 72, 168
    history of xv–xxxii, 93, 103, 120, 134–35

    Manchester Institute of Innovation Research (MIoIR) xxv, 135, 163, 169
    research, scholarship and academic journals xxv, 38, 99, 133, 135–38, 140–42, 163, 167
    role in society 95, 98, 99, 103, 133, 136, 138, 142, 160, 164–65, 167–69, 171
    transnational campuses 150
    Work and Equalities Institute 98, 100, 135, 162, 168
    see also business schools; Masood Entrepreneurship Centre; Productivity Institute
angel finance 47
Arnold, John xix, xx, xxii, xxiii, xxiv, xxv, xxvii
artificial intelligence (AI) 1, 10, 28, 37, 70–72, 88, 106–17, 123–24, 156, 168, 169
Askew, Norman xxx

173

Bank of England 44
banking sector 61–71
    open banking 62, 64, 65, 71
Banister, Nigel xxvii
Beer, Stafford xx
Bernstein, Howard (Sir) 165
'blue chip' 47, 48
Brexit 48–49, 66, 156, 162, 166
Brown, Gordon 48
Brown, Keith xxvi
business
    'big business' 6
        see also corporations and companies
    collective interest 5
    decision-making 7, 66, 68, 70
    democratisation of 7
    expectations from society 4, 83
    as a force for good 5–8
    leaders and leadership xviii, 4, 15, 38, 83–84, 87, 89, 90, 96, 162, 167, 171
        see also workplace: (line-)management
    moral obligation of 4
        see also climate change; mental health: work-related; social responsibility
    and the state 7, 22, 163
    structures 7, 21, 71
business and management studies xviii, 2, 8, 132, 133, 138
business schools
    and collaborators 2, 37, 38, 162, 164–65, 167–69
    and creativity 120–24, 126, 129–30
    and government 146–48, 149, 153, 155, 156
    history of xviii, xx
    international campuses 150, 154
    leaders 130, 139, 143
    league tables 137, 150
    research 1, 2, 8, 24, 62, 72, 90, 96, 120, 121, 126–30, 133, 137–39, 141–43, 150, 152, 154–56, 163, 167
        see also Alliance Manchester Business School: research…; University of Manchester: research
    societal impact and responsibility 1–2, 4, 8, 24, 98, 103, 141–42, 146, 148, 152–56, 160, 170–71
    structure of 8, 154, 167
    teaching 2, 8, 72, 89, 90, 96, 114, 116, 120–21, 129–30, 149, 150, 152–54, 156, 164, 167
        see also students; universities

Cameron, David 48
Cannon, Tom xx, xxi, xxii
capital 13, 15, 20, 24, 46–48, 51, 53, 55, 66–69
    human 43–44, 51
    venture 31, 47, 166
    see also market
capitalism 6
care sector 98
Channon, Derek F. 136
Chester, Teddy xvi, xvii
China 14, 16–18, 23, 149, 150
citizens see population
climate change 1, 12, 14, 15, 21, 30, 123, 128, 151, 153, 156, 163
    COP26 21
    economic opportunities 13, 24, 163
    fossil fuels 12, 16
    greenhouse gas (GHG) 12, 13, 16, **17**
    Intergovernmental Panel on Climate Change (IPCC) 12
    net zero targets 12–24, **15**, 163
    see also sustainability; technology: new technologies
community 3, 9, 36, 97, 169, 170–71
consumer 4, 13, 64–65, 69, 168
    benefits 71

Coombs, Rod xvii, xxiii, xxiv, xxv
Cooper, Cary (Sir) xvii, 10, 136
corporations and companies 21, 79, 99, 125
  and climate change 20–24
  impact on individuals 6
  power of 6
  purpose 7
  see also small and medium enterprises
COVID-19 xxvii, 64, 66, 88, 154, 161
  accelerating change 2
creative industries 34, 106, 125, 168–169
creativity 79–80, 111, 114, 116, 117, 119–130, 134
  see also business schools: and creativity; innovation
Creativity and Innovation Management 120, 135, 136
critical thinking xx, 112, 116, 170

data, use of (financial services) 61, 62–65, 67, 68, 70–72
Davies, Eddie xxxi, **plate 16**
  Eddie Davies Library xxxi, **plate 8**
debt 29, 67
deindustrialisation 43, 166
democracy 1, 169–71
Devine, Fiona xx, xxvi, xxxi–xxxii, 10, **plate 15, plate 16**
devolved governance 49, 50, 53, 54, 56
  devolved city-regions 48, 50, 51, 53–55, 57, 95, 166
  see also Manchester: Mayor of and Greater Manchester Combined Authority
Devolution White Paper, The (2024) 56
Dew, Ronald xvii
'digital multinational' 152
discriminated groups 5, 100

economy
  and democracy 1–2
  'innovation economy' 27, 28, 30, 35, 37, 39
  liberalisation 4
  macroeconomic 62–63
  monocentricity 44, 46
  Organisation for Economic Co-operation and Development (OECD) 43, 44, 51–53, 55, 57, 70, 78, 94, 122
  see also globalisation
emotional intelligence 83–85, 88, 89, 90
employment *see* labour (workforce); mental health: work-related; workplace
Employment Rights Bill 98
equality and inclusion
  in business 88, 95–97, 99, 162
  in universities 5, 112, 153, 169, 170
Europe 14, 42, 57, 63, 100
  emissions 16
  European Commission 14
  EU 23, 151, 156
  Germany xxvii, 16, 23
  Net Zero Industry Act (2023) 14
  renewable electricity 16–19

Fagan, Colette 169
Financial Conduct Authority (FCA) 21, 22
financial services 15, 62, 64–72
  financial technology (FinTech) 61–63, 71–72, 168
  see also innovation: digital *and* financial
Ford, Henry 124
Franks, Lord xviii–xix
Franks Report (1963) xix, 132
FTSE 100 21, 46

Gen Z 30
geopolitical tensions 10, 88, 146, 151, 154, 162

Georghiou, Luke xxv, 93, 134, 163
gender pay gap 88
Gilbert, Alan xxv, xxx
globalisation 4, 44, 63, 148–50, 162
   see also 'slowbalisation'
Goldin, Claudia 100
Goodman, John xvii
Gove, Michael 48
governance triangle 146, **147**, 149, 151, 152, 156
government, UK 21, 22, 44, 46, 48, 49, 53, 55, 56, 94, 132, 139, 156, 163, 165, 168, 171
   centralisation 44, 46, 47, 49–50, 166
   Labour Government, the (2024–) 9, 23, 27, 29, 111
   local 52, 54, 165
   (mis)trust in 3, 4, 169–70
   policy *see* policy(making)
   see also devolved governance; *former Prime Ministers*
Green, Ken xxiv

Hague, Douglas xvii
Haldane, Andy 48, 50
Hampson, Diana xxxi
Hankins, Harold xxix
health sector 30, 34, 37, 77, 98, 106, 107–11, 114, 161, 167, 169
   see also care sector; National Health Service
Hollier, Bob xvii
housing sector 55, 69, 161
human rights 7, 170

industrialisation *see* deindustrialisation
industry disaster 7
information and communication technology (ICT) 62–65, 70, 71
innovation
   digital 61–62, 106
   ecosystem 9, 10, 31, 34–37, 164

financial 64–72, 163
healthcare 34, 108, 114, 169
Manchester Institute of Innovation Research (MIoIR) xxv, 38, 135, 163, 169
partnerships 37, 39
race to 14, 20–21, 23
regional 29, 30, 33, 34, 36, 38, 39, 51, 103
students 30–32, 36–37
teaching 24, 120, 125, 126, 164
University of Manchester (UoM) 27–28, 30, 33–39, 134–35, 163
workplace 79, 90
see also technology: new technology; University of Manchester: Unit M
interdisciplinarity 161, 167–169, 171
International Monetary Fund (IMF) 13
investment
   foreign (global) 37, 46, 51, 53, 54
   regional 42, 48, 50, 53–55, 57

Japan 47, 57
Jevons, Stanley xvii, xxv
'junk bond' 47

Kent, A. F. xvi

labour (workforce) 6, 44, 55, 56, 71, 72, 77, 82, 86, 88, 102, 162
   market 96, 99–101, 103
   wages (pay) 5, 39, 82, 94, 98, 102, 103
   gender pay gap 88
   women 100
   see also Employment Rights Bill; mental health: work-related; productivity: worker; skills; workplace
Langrish, John 134, 135
Levelling Up 48

living standards 29, 94–95, 99, 101–103, 161
London xviii, xxiv, 41–48, 50–52, 135
  versus national regions 57, 94, 101, 166
  see also government: centralisation; UK: South(-East)
Luger, Mike xx, xxv, xxvi, xxx
Lupton, Tom xx, xxi, 134

Madinani, Vikram xxvi
Manchester (Greater)
  businesses and investment 31–33, 37, 99–102
  economy 3, 31, 34, 36, 39, 53, 94, 95, 103, 115
  Greater Manchester Combined Authority 37, 53–54, 57, 95, 98, 103, 164–65, 166
    Good Employment Charter 98, 102
    see also Alliance Manchester Business School; devolved governance; University of Manchester
  history of xxiv, xxvi
  local authorities 33, 37, 94, 166
  Mayor of (Andy Burnham) 29, 33, 37, 166
  Oxford Road xxx, 33
  social challenges 30, 101–2, 103
  see also innovation: ecosystem; UK: North(-West); University of Manchester
Manchester Method, The xx–xxi, xxvi, 152
Marchington, Mick 97
Marett, Sean xxvii
market
  competition 20–21, 23, 45, 56, 64, 65, 67, 71, **147**, 148, 152
  deregulated 45
  global 45, 71, 148, 150, 151
  local and domestic 53, 148

new 21, 163
risk xxiv, 48
structures 63
see also 2008 global financial crisis; banking sector; capital
Masood Entrepreneurship Centre, The xxxi, 38, 163
McClelland, Grigor xix–xx, xxi, 136
McPhail, Ken xx, xxvi, xxxii
mental health
  stigma 77–78
  work-related 77–90, 100, 161, 162
    absence from work 78
    job loss 77
    role of manager 80–85, 88–89
    wellbeing metrics 85–88, 90
    work–life 79, 82
  see also workplace
mergers and acquisitions (M&A) 67, 70, 71
Metcalfe, Stan xxv
Moore, S. A. xxii
Mumford, Enid xx, 134

nationalism 4, 146, 162
National Health Service (NHS) 108, 169

Osborne, George 48

Pearson, Alan xxv, 134
pension funds 68–69
Pettigrew, Andrew 134
policy(making) 8, 136–39, 143, 170
  absence of 166
  economic 44, 48, 69, 166
  government 44, 45, 49, 95, 101, 146, 149, 156, 163
  industrial 20, 94
  innovation 13, 21, 38, 135
  trade 4
  university 133, 135, 162, 171

population
  disempowered and disadvantaged 4, 65
  migration 4, 43
  sizes 42–43, 47, 51, 52, 53
populism 4, 6, 151, 156, 170
poverty and inequality 94–96, 103, 128, 151, 156, 162
productivity
  gap 52, 101, 103
  growth 13, 35–36, 56, 63, 65, 69–72, 94, 101, 156
  low 31, 41, 43, 47, 49–52, 57, 79, 98, 99, 102, 161–62, 165
  national 49–51, 94–95, 99, 100
  regional 34, 39, 41–44, 45, 46, 50–52, 94, 101, 102, 165–66
  worker 10, 38, 63, 70, 72, 79–81, 84, 89, 90, 97, 99, 100, 162
  see also labour (workforce)
Productivity Institute, The (TPI) 31, 38, 70, 98, 99, 135, 162
public, the 13, 49, 170
public services 29, 94, 95
publication 3, 121–22, 126–29, 136–41
  see also Alliance Manchester Business School: research…; research

quantitative easing (QE) 48

recruitment xviii, 81, 85, 96, 97
  see also labour (workforce); workplace: staff turnover
research
  research and development (R&D) xxv, 28, 31–37, 54, 67, 115, 125, 134–35, 151
  Research Excellence Framework (REF) xxiv, 133, 140–41
  Responsible Research in Business and Management (RRBM) 142

San Francisco Declaration on Research Assessment (DORA) 141
societal impact 3, 140, 141–42
Vision of Responsible Research in Business and Management, A 142
  see also business schools; publication; universities; University of Manchester
Revans, Reginald 'Reg' xvi, xx
Rickards, Tudor xx, xxvi, 120, 134–35
Robbins, Lord xviii, 93
Rogers, Carl R. 119–20
Rothwell, Nancy xxvi
Rubery, Jill xvii
Rutherford, Ernest xvi, 27

Saville, Peter xxvi
science, technology and innovation, study of 38, 135
Scotland 46, 47, 56
shareholders 5, 67, 68, 71, 83–86, 91, 99, 133
skills
  development and learning 4, 24, 33, 38, 51, 53, 72, 88, 90, 100, 102, 112, 115
  digital 111
  leadership 38, 72, 82, 89, 90
  life 2, 170, 171
  shortage 32, 35, 39, 56, 71, 101
  Skills England 29
  workers' under-utilised skills 78, 100
'slowbalisation' 151–54, 156
small and medium enterprises (SMEs) 28, 32, 39, 51, 54, 65, 72, 164–65
social media 3, 106, 151, 170, 172
social responsibility xix, 4, 34, 35, 99, 152, 155

state, the
  and business 7
  regulation of 6
  see also government
start-ups and scale-ups 28, 32, 35–39, 54, 61, 114, 167
stock shares, bonds and dividends 47, 67–69, 71, 91
students
  agents of change 172
  and AI 112, 114, 124
  experience of 10, 30, 39
  and entrepreneurship xxxi, 9, 30, 32, 36, 38, 163–65
  international xxi, xxvii, 149, 154, 156
  see also business schools: creativity *and* teaching; Gen Z; universities
supply chains 4, 6, 13, **15**, 34, 54, 56, 124, 125
sustainability 28, 36, 83, 99, 133, 146, 151–55, 168
  International Sustainability Standards Board (ISSB) 22–23
  metrics 21–25
  United Nations Sustainable Development Goals (SDGs) 28, 99, 153, 156
  see also climate change

tax 53, 69, 152
technology
  (lack of) access to 112, 156, 170
  biotech 37
  new technologies 13–20, 23, 29–30, 51, 62, 71, 72, 95, 98, 134, 155, 163, 164
    electric vehicles (EV) 12–14, **15,** 18–21, 23
    ethical challenges 35, 107, 114
    renewable energy 12–14, 16, **17,** 18–21, **20**, 23

  see also climate change: greenhouse gas; net zero targets
  and productivity 13, 70–72, 108
  resistance to change 134
  role in society 107
  see also artificial intelligence; information and communication technology; financial services: FinTech
Telfer, Rab xx, xxi
trade 4, 6, 44, 55–56, 148
transport 12, 13, 44, 51, 55
Treasury, HM 13, 21, 49, 94

UK, the
  economic and social challenges 29, 41–43, 94, 99, 165–66
  Midlands, the 56, 57
  see devolved governance
  national versus regional growth 49, 51–52
  North(-West), the 28, 29, 31, 39, 41, 44, 46, 50, 54, 56, 57, 94, 164, 166
  see also devolved governance; Manchester: Greater Manchester Combined Authority
  pan-regional growth 41, 45, 54, 57
  regional inequalities 48–49, 94, 165–66
  regional migration 43–44
  South(-East), the 44, 46–47, 52, 56, 57, 166
  see also London
Ulph, Alistair xxiii
universities
  business models of 2
  engagement with communities 2, 4–5, 103, 170–71
  internationalisation of 150–51
  rankings (league tables) 137, 139, 150

responsibilities of 3, 4, 170
role in society 2, 3, 29, 135, 170
see also business schools: research; publication; research; students; University of Manchester
University of Manchester (UoM) 28–30, 33–37, 99
  history of xv–xxxii, 27, 93, 103, 133–35
  research 133–36, 141
  role in society 3, 34, 95, 102, 136, 155, 164, 167
  Unit M 28–29, 31, 36–38, 103, 163
  see also Alliance Manchester Business School; *individual institutes*
US, the 14, 51, 53, 57, 63, 67, 70, 161
  business schools xviii, xxv
  emissions and energy technologies 14, 16–18, **19**
  presidency and administration 12, 14, 151, 162

Wales 46, 56
Walker, Martin xxiv
Ward, Adolphus William 119
Wealth from Knowledge 135
wellbeing *see* mental health
Whitley, Richard 134
Williams, Bruce xvii, xxiv
Wilson, Harold 93
Wood, Doug xxvii
Work and Equalities Institute 98, 100, 135, 162, 168
workplace 63, 80–82, 88, 134, 168
  hybrid working 81, 82, 85
  human resources (HR) 81, 82, 85, 88, 97
  job satisfaction 82, 85, 90, 134
  (line-)management 81–82, 85, 88
    see also mental health: work-related: role of manager
  staff turnover 79, 84, 87, 90
  organisation's culture 81, 84, 90
  see also productivity: worker; mental health: work-related